Sex/Gender

This book provides a clearly written explanation of the biological and cultural underpinnings of sex/gender. Anne Fausto-Sterling provides an introduction to the biochemistry, neurobiology, and social construction of sex/gender with expertise and humor in a style accessible to a wide variety of readers. In addition to the basics, *Sex/Gender* ponders the moral, ethical, social, and political side to this inescapable subject.

Anne Fausto-Sterling, the Nancy Duke Lewis Professor of Biology and Gender Studies at Brown University, is a leading expert on the development of gender identity as well as the biology of gender. Her latest research analyzes the emergence of behavioral differences between the sexes in early childhood. She is the author of two earlier books: *Myths of Gender: Biological Theories about Women and Men* (Basic, 1993) and *Sexing the Body: Gender Politics and the Construction of Sexuality* (Basic, 2000).

The Routledge Series Integrating Science and Culture

Editor: Lennard J. Davis, University of Illinois at Chicago

The Routledge Series Integrating Science and Culture aims to reunite the major discourses of science and the humanities which parted ways about 150 years ago. Each book picks an important topic that can best be understood by a synthesis of the best science and the best social and cultural analysis. In an age when more and more major political and life decisions involve complex understandings of science, medicine, and technology, we need to have a bioculturally sophisticated citizenry who can weigh in on these important issues. To that end these books aim to reach a wide swathe of people, presenting the information in readable, illustrated, succinct editions that are designed for classroom and scholarly use as well as for public consumption.

Available
Autism by Stuart Murray
Depression by Bradley Lewis

Forthcoming
Culture by Nicole Anderson
Brain, Self, and Society by Victoria Pitts-Taylor

Sex/Gender

Biology in a Social World

Anne Fausto-Sterling

 Routledge
Taylor & Francis Group

NEW YORK AND LONDON

Please visit the book's companion website at
www.routledge.com/cw/fausto-sterling

This edition published 2012
by Routledge
711 Third Avenue, New York, NY 10017

Simultaneously published in the UK
by Routledge
2 Park Square, Milton Park, Abingdon, Oxon OX14 4RN

Routledge is an imprint of the Taylor & Francis Group, an informa business

Library of Congress Cataloging in Publication Data
Fausto-Sterling, Anne, 1944–
Sex/gender: biology in a social world / Anne Fausto-Sterling.
    p. cm. — (The Routledge Series integrating science and culture)
1. Sex differences. 2. Gender identity. 3. Sex differentiation. 4. Intersexuality.
5. Sex (Biology). 6. Sex role. I. Title.
HQ1075.F387 2012
305.3—dc23

                                                              2011040011

ISBN: 978–0–415–88145–6 (hbk)
ISBN: 978–0–415–88146–3 (pbk)
ISBN: 978–0–203–12797–1 (ebk)

Typeset in Adobe Caslon Pro
by RefineCatch Limited, Bungay, Suffolk, UK

Printed and bound in the United States of America by
Edwards Brothers, Inc., Lillington, North Carolina

This book is dedicated to Samuel Philip and
Rebecca Claire Graves and to Carl Luke Vogel. They
are the ones who will reshape the future of gender-in-the-world.

CONTENTS

SERIES FOREWORD

The Routledge Series Integrating Science and Culture aims to restore connections between the sciences and the humanities, connections that were severed over 150 years ago. This mutual exclusion was done in the name of expertise on the part of science and defended in the name of preserving values and morality in the world of humanism. In some sense, each side was seen as the societal enemy of the other. From the humanists' perspective, scientists threatened to make the world a colder, more efficient place lacking in feelings and values. From the scientists' viewpoint, humanists were interfering with progress by injecting bleeding hearts and unreasonable fears into an essentially rational process.

But the reality is that now, in the 21st century it is getting harder and harder for humanists to comment on civic and social matters without knowing something about science, medicine, and technology. Suddenly there is the need to understand stem cells, brain scans, DNA technologies, organ transplants, ecological outcomes, and the like in order to be a knowledgeable citizen, legislator, or scholar. Likewise, scientists routinely include the ethical, social, cultural, and legal in their research protocols and scientific articles. The divide between the "two cultures" described by C. P. Snow in the 1950s is less and less possible in the 21st century. On the ground, humanists and scientists are again in need of each other.

To that end, the books in this series will focus on the cultural side of science and the scientific side of culture. David Morris and I have coined the term "biocultural" to indicate this new realm of study and critique. In that spirit, Anne Fausto-Sterling's book helps us think about the topics of gender and sexuality in ways that make it impossible to ever consider these subjects as independent from a social-cultural matrix. Yet, Fausto-Sterling also makes it impossible to think of the very same subject as independent from a biological endowment, as well. The genius of this book is that it exploits the author's expertise as both a biologist and a social-cultural analyst. Given her knowledge of cell biology and gender studies, Fausto-Sterling brings to the series a layered, nuanced, and complex view of something that many people consider simple. But while you may be able to sex a puppy rather easily, the complex role of gender in human culture, biology, and psychology needs more investigation than just a casual glance. This book—to the point, humorous, and wise—provides the best introduction to the field that I can imagine.

Lennard J. Davis
Series Editor

PREFACE

One reason I rarely attend large parties with many strangers is that I hate it when people ask me what I do. As soon as I say I'm a biologist, my interlocutor winces, falls silent, or murmurs something about having done badly in high school biology. I get these responses from highly accomplished academics in the humanities and social sciences. As I said, I hate this. My conversation partner may think all biology is irrelevant to the great philosophical issues of the world—equality, suffering, hunger, etc. Or he or she may feel that biology is an urgent subject, but one he or she feels too inadequate to discuss. I, on the other hand, feel that biology holds one (not the only—by a long shot) approach to understanding critical world issues *and* that anyone interested enough to pay attention can learn to read and interpret biology with a suitably critical eye.

What do I mean by a suitably critical eye? We encounter many misuses of biology—oversimplifications of research findings about the origins of human sexuality or claims that biological difference explains differences in achievement or other large inequalities. This makes it all the more important that students of the humanities and the social sciences learn a form of biology that provides them with tools to analyze these aspects of the world. And so, when Lennard Davis, the general editor of the series in which this book appears, wrote me with a proposal to write a *short* book on sex and gender for *The Routledge Series Integrating Science and Culture* I jumped at the chance.

As I understood my task, I was to write a brief treatment about biology, sex, and gender; the book was to place our current biological knowledge in an historical and cultural framework. The aim was to provide interested readers with a way to understand and think critically about at least some of what they hear in the popular press and in casual conversation about sex and gender. Lennard Davis also asked that I analyze the state of our knowledge. What do we know? What do we think we know? What might we be able to find out in the future? What questions might be impossible to answer? And I confess to having a secret goal—to convey my own enthusiasm for the study of the biological world—the worms and flies as well as the humans.

This book should find a place as a companion text in general science courses, introductory biology and psychology courses, gender studies courses, and a variety of introductory and more specialized courses in psychology, sociology, anthropology, and the humanities. Instructors in such courses face certain types of problems. Issues arise that are outside of the instructor's realm of expertise. Or, the standard texts that address biology and gender are insufficiently critical or fail to integrate information into a broader social and historical context. Or, they talk down to the learners (in this case instructor and student alike), using what feminist scholar Donna Haraway calls the God-Trick—speaking from everywhere and nowhere at the same time. This book might provide concise approaches that would help the instructor and students join together to investigate biological aspects of the question of gender together.

In the case of the "straight" science courses the comprehensive required text is dry, weighs a lot more than the modern laptop, and overwhelms students with its presentation of fact after fact. Usually such facts remain unattached to what students find important in daily life. Perhaps a short, focused book about a topic of great interest to youthful students (sex!!), written with a little humor, and a gloss on certain details might help. The biologists and psychologists will have to be patient with the fact that I sometimes use popular language rather than precise scientific terminology. This is the privilege of the popular science writer. Of course, sociologists will want more sociology in this book, anthropologists more anthropology, and psychologists more psychology. That's what the

Further Reading section at the end of each chapter is for. And, of course, different instructors and lay readers are likely to bring some of their own strengths to the reading experience. They can fill in bits that I left out.

In *Sex/Gender: Biology in a Social World* I try to build a method of analysis that readers can use now and in the future as they consider questions of biology. The most important tenet is "don't get stuck trying to divide nature from nurture." Instead, think developmentally. Remember that living bodies are dynamic systems that develop and change in response to their social and historical contexts. This is as true for rodents as it is for humans. And appreciate biological diversity. Just because rats do gender one way, doesn't mean that prairie voles or Japanese macaques or humans do it the same way. To me, one of the wonders of the natural world is its biological diversity.

I have striven for a lively read. For this reason some of my chapters are very short, making a single interesting point. Others are longer but sometimes with short sections. I emphasize biology, but I tie matters to sociological and cultural processes (although these latter are not the main focus of the book). Finally, the chapter sequence is organized roughly, as a developmental sequence, based on sex/gender as it unfolds from fertilization through early childhood. At the very end, I turn more topical with chapters on human sexuality and on childhood sex differences.

To access color versions of selected figures in this text, readers of the electronic version of this book can make use of hyperlinks embedded in the URLs in the captions, where indicated. Readers of the traditional, print-based version can access the same web pages by referring to the URLs and directions given.

Last, but not least, I want to acknowledge the generous and prompt help from Lennard Davis, series editor, the Routledge editors Steven Rutter and Leah Babb-Rosenfeld, and those who reviewed the book: Judith Howard at the University of Washington, Sally Raskoff at Los Angeles Valley College, and Marianna Litovich at Wesleyen College. Most importantly, my wife Paula A. Vogel enthusiastically read the entire manuscript as I produced it and helped me to feel that I was on the right track. As with most things in life, I couldn't do these projects without her love and support.

1

A GENDERLESS FUTURE?

What were they thinking! In March, 2010 the New South Wales (Australia) Registry of Births, Deaths and Marriages sent Scottish-born Norrie May-Welby an immigration certificate listing her as "sex not specified." The bureaucratic decision to allow May-Welby to immigrate without specifying his/her sex or gender came after an extended legal battle. As it turned out, May-Welby's official genderless-ness was a way station in a struggle that continues as of this writing. Following intense publicity, the Registry backtracked, claiming it did not have legal authority to produce a gender neutral certificate. May-Welby is suing. Moreover, May-Welby is not the only person on earth who wishes to live gender free. Reporters Barbara Kantrowitz and Pat Wingert suggest that a growing number of people consider themselves gender neutral (Kantrowitz & Wingert, 2010).

Confusion about gender categories (Male? Female? Neither? Both?) seems to be perennially newsworthy. Take the case of the South African runner Caster Semenya. During the summer of 2009, she beat the women's 800-meter running record by several seconds. Although her achievement remained a good 18 seconds off the men's record, her breakthrough prompted complaints that Ms. Semenya was really a man. An international scandal erupted when the International Association of

Athletics Federations (IAAF), track and field's governing body, barred her from competition until she completed a gender test.

A what? What on earth is a gender test? You might think it is simple to tell who is male and who is female. Indeed, sometimes it *is* simple. But not always. More than a year into this story the IAAF decided to allow Semenya to resume competition. In August of 2010 she won handily in women's races in Berlin, Germany and in June 2011 she came in third in competition in Oslo, Norway ("Bolt Blitz in Oslo; Athletics," 2011). But the IAAF did *not* release the gender test results, rightly maintaining that these contain Caster Semenya's personal and very private health information. So we remain in the dark about what a gender test actually is and how, in this case, it gave the IAAF the information it needed to allow Semenya to resume competition (Caster Semenya, 2010).

Genderless Australian immigrants. Record breaking runners who may not really be women. What then, are we to think about the future of gender? Is it really disappearing (I doubt it); should there be more than two legal gender categories (possibly); do we know enough about sex and gender to deal intelligently with the idea of a genderless future (no)? After all, don't chromosomes that join together at fertilization fix sex and gender for a lifetime (no)? Don't societies all think (more or less) the same way about sex and gender (no)? Have they always thought the same way about sex and gender (and no again)? Perhaps there are things about sex and gender that we can never know. And if so why can't we know them? These are among the questions this book addresses. Perhaps you thought you already knew what sex was, what gender was, and all of the essentials about human sexuality. And perhaps so. But in this book I start at the beginning with developing embryos and explore what we know about sex and gender and how well we know it. Then, based on the knowledge gained, maybe we can look at the future of gender, if not definitively, perhaps and at least, intelligently.

2
OF SPIRALS AND LAYERS

Where Do We Start?

There is no right place. Do we begin with the story of boy meets girl (or girl buys sperm at a sperm bank?), the development of eggs and sperms, or the more traditional moment of fertilization (sperm fuses with egg)? No matter what point we choose, we start in the middle of the story of sex and gender; from there we can race forward, and end up looping back (Figure 2.1). For now, let's start with a traditional framework, fill in some of the things we currently know about the biology of sex development, and then loop back to offer some interesting tidbits that complicate the basic story just a bit.

In the 1950s psychologist John Money and his colleagues at Johns Hopkins University pioneered the study of sexually ambiguous patients. As he worked with children and some adults born into the world with unusual combinations of sex markers (testes and a vagina, ovaries and a penis, two X chromosomes and a scrotum, and more) Money developed a layered model of sex and gender (Figure 2.2). He started with fertilization. Human males produce two kinds of sperm—one with an X chromosome plus one each of so-called autosomes, and the other with a Y chromosome and one each of the so-called autosomes. Later (Chapter 3), I will discuss what we know about how the X, the Y, and

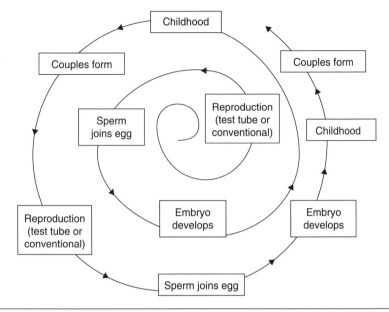

Figure 2.1 Sex spiral.

the autosomes contribute to the development of sex. But for now, let's stay focused on the bigger framework. At the same time that the male produces X- or Y-bearing sperm, females, having two X chromosomes, produce only one kind of egg—X-bearing with a full set of autosomes. Egg and sperm join forces. The result is a double set of autosomes plus an X and a Y or a double set of autosomes plus two Xs. Voilà! We have what Money called *chromosomal sex*-layer 1 in the multilayered phyllo dough (or for those of Germanic extraction—strüdel) pastry we call sex-gender.

Usually, about 8 weeks after conception, embryos with a Y chromosome develop an embryonic testis and by 12 weeks, those with two Xs form embryonic ovaries. Once a developing fetus has gonads (the general term for testes or ovaries) it has, by definition acquired *fetal gonadal sex*. The fetal gonads quickly get down to business and start making hormones important to the embryo's progress. Again, I will circle back with details in the next chapter. But for now, all we need to know is that once the fetal gonadal hormones appear we can say that the

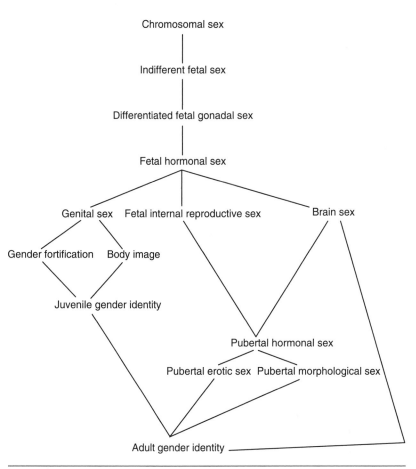

Figure 2.2 Layers of sex.

fetus has acquired a *fetal hormonal sex*. Fetal hormonal sex contributes to the formation of the *internal reproductive sex* (the uterus, cervix, and Fallopian tubes in females and the vas deferens, prostate, and epididymis in males). As the fetus nears the end of its fourth month of development, fetal hormones complete their job of shaping the external genitalia (*genital sex*)—penis and scrotum in males, vagina and clitoris in females. By birth, then, baby has five layers of sex. And, as we shall see, these layers do not always agree with one another (Gilbert, 2010).

But we have only begun to layer. At birth, Money and his colleagues pointed out, the adults surrounding the newborn identified sex based on their perception of external genital anatomy (genital dimorphism); this identification initiated a social response that began the *gender* socialization of the newborn. Note the hand off from sex to gender. Money and others use gender to designate an individual identity or self presentation (Green, 2010; Money & Ehrhardt, 1972). These are always structured to be specific to a particular culture. For example, in the United States a masculine or male-presenting woman would wear pants, have short hair, and refrain from using make-up. In contrast to most psychologists, many sociologists use gender to refer to social structures that differentiate men from women (Lorber, 1994). These might seem to be relatively innocuous, for example, separate public bathrooms, or a requirement that we designate our sex on official documents such as passports or driver's licenses. Or they might really restrict one's freedom, as, for example, laws that forbid women to drive or vote.

Table 2.1 Lorber's subdivision of gender

As a social institution, *gender is composed of:*	*For an* individual, *gender is composed of:*
Gender statuses: socially recognized genders and expectations for their enactment behaviorally, gesturally, linguistically, emotionally, and physically	*Sex category:* individual assigned prenatally, at birth, or following reconstructive surgery
Gendered division of labor	*Gender identity:* the individual's sense of gendered self as a worker and family member
Gendered kinship: the family rights and responsibilities for each gender status	*Gendered marital and procreative status:* fulfillment or nonfulfillment of allowed or disallowed mating, impregnation, childbearing, and/or kinship roles

Gendered sexual scripts: the normative patterns of sexual desire and sexual behavior as prescribed for different gender statuses

Gendered sexual orientation: socially and individually patterned sexual desires, feelings, practices, and identifications

Gendered personalities: combinations of traits patterned by gendered behavioral norms for different gender statuses

Gendered personality: internalized patterns of socially normative emotions as organized by family structure and parenting

Gendered social control: the formal and informal approval and reward of conforming behavior and stigmatization and medicalization of nonconforming behavior

Gendered processes: "doing gender"—the social practices of learning and enacting gender-appropriate behaviors, i.e. of developing a gender identity

Gender ideology: the justification of gender statuses, often by invoking arguments about natural (biological) difference

Gender beliefs: incorporation of, or resistance to, gender ideology

Gender imagery: the cultural representations of gender in symbolic language and artistic productions

Gender display: presentation of self as a kind of gendered person through dress, cosmetics, adornments, and permanent and reversible body markers

Source: Adapted from Lorber (1994: 30–31)

I will use "gender" in both senses, but whenever I refer to the body and/or individual behaviors, I will use the term "sex." An individual, therefore, has a sex (male, female, not designated, other); but they engage with the world via a variety of social, gender conventions. Each individual, thus, manufactures a gender presentation that can feed back on the individual's sex, and is interpreted by others using the specific gender frameworks of an individual's culture. Gender, then, is definitely in the eye of the beholder. Sex *and* gender presentation are in the body *and* mind of the presenter.

But back to newborns. The social response to the genital sex of the newborn is intense. Consider two markers—clothing and toys. Artist

JeongMee Yoon has engaged in a several year project rendering images of children's pink and blue things. In Figure 2.3 Yoon presents us with Lauren and Carolyn's pink things and Ethan's blue things (Yoon, 2006). Well, to be honest, if you are holding a print version of this book in your hands, the images are in black and white. But if you go to the book's website at www.routledge.com/cw/fausto-sterling you can see the full color effect of these works of art. The images hold a lot of information. Not only is the intensity of the color scheme striking; noteworthy as well is the preponderance of clothing, dolls, and stuffed animals

Figure 2.3 (a) Lauren and Carolyn and Their Pink Things 2006, by JeongMee Yoon (http://www.jeongmeeyoon.com/aw_pinkblue.htm).

For color versions of these figures please go to www.routledge.com/cw/fausto-sterling

Figure 2.3 (b) Ethan and His Blue Things 2006, by JeongMee Yoon (http://www.jeongmeeyoon.com/aw_pinkblue.htm).

among Lauren and Carolyn's things. This contrasts with the tools, sports equipment, and trucks in Ethan's possession.

What options do parents have when they start buying or accepting gifts for their newborns? Consider the Babies'r Us website[1], which categorizes infant clothing as baby girl, baby boy, or neutral. Whereas the main theme of gender neutrality seems to be yellow baby ducks, newborn outfits for boys sport blue, brown, green, white, or black clothing with a monkey or sports themes. Newborn girl outfits sport purple, pink or pink trimmed, pastel light greens, or white colors with flower logos. The rare neutral infant suit was white with a giraffe logo.

The toys section had more overlap in items said to be for either a boy or a girl. But the differentiation remains clear. Although there are no designated gender neutral toys, both boy and girl toy categories featured the same Baby Einstein products. But the boys' page also featured a large variety of trucks, and the *New York Yankees ABC My First Alphabet Book* (2009). To be fair, the girls also had some trucks, albeit in neutral, yellow, or "girl-colored," i.e. pink, vehicles. Other girlie offers included a *Leap Frog Cook* and *Play Potsy Toy* and a Fischer Price *Little People Nativity Playset*. Money dryly refers to all this pinkish, bluish hullabaloo as "other's response" but I think it merits a better name: *gender fortification*.

Infants are born to explore the world. They start by assimilating information from the senses. They sense touch, warmth, light, and sound. They experience hunger and feeding. They hear their own crying and experience a caregiver's response. They respond to the discomfort of a wet, full diaper, and experience sensations as an adult cleans, dries, and powders their genitals, perineum, and anal area. From these simple beginnings infants develop a sense of their own body, a sensory body image. The anatomy of the external genitalia affects this developing body image, and this is yet another level of sexual formation—*the sex of the body image* (see Figure 2.2).

But wait! There's more! Money links one more layer of sex to *fetal gonadal sex*, something he calls brain dimorphism, and I am calling *brain sex*. I will say at the outset that there is a great deal of argument about what brain sex is, whether it is real, if so when it develops, and what it might mean for the development of males and females (Fausto-Sterling, 2000; Fine, 2010; Jordan-Young, 2010), and again I will return to this in Chapter 4. But Money's paradigm of brain sex dominates the thinking of most scientists who study gender differences, and so I put it on the table from the beginning.

To recap: a newborn is a multilayered sexual creature, the result of having a chromosomal sex, a fetal gonadal sex, fetal hormonal sex, a fetal internal reproductive sex, a brain sex (of which more later), an external genital sex, and, starting from the moment the child leaves the womb, a developing body image and social gender fortification. Money and his colleagues suggest that this entire list of "sexes" combine to produce a youngster's sense of self as male or female, something they call *juvenile gender identity*. Finally, at puberty, the gonads which differentiated during fetal development become active, creating yet another layer— *pubertal hormonal sex*. These "raging hormones" of the pre-teen and teen years influence the development of erotic sensations and desires (*pubertal erotic sex*) and adult sex-differentiated anatomy—what Money called *pubertal morphological sex*. All of these different sexes and identities in turn converge to produce *adult gender identity*, the sense of self as an adult male or an adult female.

It's a neat scheme; a little complicated, to be sure, but still containing nice neat lines. All a person has to do is navigate these developmental paths and the end result is clear—either a person who is self-evidently male, or one who is self-evidently female develops. Nice, until we realize that each of the layers can, potentially, develop independently of one another. This doesn't happen very often, but when it does, a child can be born who is a genuine mixture (sometimes called an intersex)—XX with a penis and scrotum, XY with well developed breasts, and other examples (Blackless, Charuvastra, Derryck, Fausto-Sterling, Lauzanne, & Lee, 2000). What happens to the developing gender identity of such people is not totally predictable, a topic to which we return in Chapter 4. But first, a little more of the basic biology.

Further Reading

Dreger, A. D. (1998). *Hermaphrodites and the Medical Invention of Sex*. Cambridge, MA: Harvard University Press.

Epstein, Brad M. (2009). *New York Yankees ABC My First Alphabet Book*. Aliso Viejo, CA:. Michaelson Entertainment.

Karkazis, K. (2008). *Fixing Sex: Intersex, Medical Authority and Lived Experience*. Durham, NC: Duke University Press.

Kessler, S. (1998). *Lessons from the Intersexed*. New Brunswick, NJ: Rutgers University Press.

Kessler, S. J., & McKenna, W. (1978). *Gender: An Ethnomethodological Approach*. New York: John Wiley & Sons.

Lorber, J. (1994). *Paradoxes of Gender*. New Haven, CT: Yale University Press.

Preves, S. E. (2003). *Intersex and Identity: the Contested Self*. New Brunswick, NJ: Rutgers University Press.

Stoller, R. (1992). *Presentations of Gender*. New Haven, CT: Yale University Press.

3

OF MOLECULES AND SEX

Variety is the Spice of Life

Scholars have written tomes on the subject of variation in animal approaches to sex/reproduction (see, for example, Bagemihl, 1999; Bell, 2008). There are lizards (and lots of insects) that don't use males at all (Crews & Fitzgerald, 1980). Instead females kick-start embryonic development without fertilization, using a process called parthenogenesis (literally "virgin birth"). There are insects that have three sexes,[1] and there are fish that have four different types of sexual beings.

Take, for example, the bluegill sunfish, a common resident of northern freshwater lakes and ponds. In the spring males build shallow, circular nests and circle repeatedly around the nest rim in order to attract a female. When she is enticed, both circle the nest at right angles to one another before resting and each depositing his (sperm) or her (eggs) contribution to the next generation of bluegills. Fertilization is external—females lay eggs in a watery nest and males swim over the eggs, layer sperm on top and hope for the best. In the afterglow, the females swim off while the males stay to aerate the nests with their tails, guard the eggs and fry, and possibly attract other females. Or at least that is the Mother Goose version of the story.

In the grown up version there are three types of males: so-called parental or bourgeois males that mature late in the game (after age 7 years), are relatively large, and have display colors. These parental males build nests, encourage passing females to lay eggs in the nests, fertilize the eggs, and then take care of the resulting offspring. A second type—bluegill sneaker males—develop young. They are the smallest males, and manage to fertilize eggs by darting in when the bourgeois males and females are going at it. All they need do is mix in some of their own sperm and, since there are lots of eggs, they manage to gain some fertilizations. Finally, satellite males mimic females in order to join spawning pairs. When sneaker males grow they can turn into satellite males using a developmental pathway that differs from that of the large bourgeois male (Godwin, 2010; Gross & Charnov, 1980).

While some fish species have several types of males, others can change completely from male to female or vice versa. In itself, this fact is astonishing, but even more amazingly, the fishes' social context controls the transformation. Consider the brightly colored reef fish called a cleaner wrasse. These smaller fish hang out in designated spots on coral reefs forming little cleaning stations. Larger fish stop by and the wrasses clean off and eat the parasites hanging onto the big fish. A commensal time is had by all. The wrasse groups consist of one or a small number of males with a dominance hierarchy and a large group of females of different sizes. If the dominant male dies or a mad scientist removes it from the group, the largest female senses the change in context and in a matter of days it transforms into a reproductively active male. This fishy ability to change sex extends to 7 taxonomic families, 27 orders, and many more species (Godwin, 2010).

Although scientists have studied socially determined sex change in fish since the early 1970s, there is still a lot we don't know about how it works. We *do* know that brain signals influence the hypothalamus and the pituitary gland which in turn notify the gonads that they should shift gears. When female wrasses sense the loss of the male their ovaries stop functioning, and as the future eggs degenerate, the gonad begins making testosterone and other hormones needed to produce a testis, and ultimately sperm. But what we don't know is pretty essential: how do events in the social sphere become events taking place in an individual body? Are the social clues that reorient the nervous system visual, auditory, mechanical, or something we haven't yet conceptualized? These questions can certainly be investigated experimentally, and answers will provide clues as to how information crosses that border from the outside to the inside of an organism.

Social interactions determine sex in certain fish; O.K. that probably seems strange. But in many reptiles it is the temperature at which fertilized eggs incubate that selects for either male or female development. Just as surprising is how this story differs from one species to the next. For example, grow the eggs of a red-eared slider turtle at 26°C and all the resultant hatchlings are male; grow the eggs at 31°C and they all come out female. In order to obtain an all female clutch of American alligators, (very carefully) obtain eggs and grow them either at 30° or at 35°C. Or—still being very careful—grab a handful and grow them at 32.5° to 33°C and voilà—you will get all males. Finally, consider the leopard gecko. For these lizards, males develop at the higher temperatures (31–33°C) and females at the lower temperatures (23–28°C).

The "dazzling array" (Shoemaker & Crews, 2009: 294) of approaches to sexual reproduction found in vertebrates is called *primary sex determination*. Many vertebrates—including humans—use chromosomal (sometimes called genotypic) sex determination: a heritable genetic element attached to a chromosome usually directs development down one of two pathways. In humans and many mammals this special element is a gene found on the Y chromosome and it pushes the embryo to develop in a male direction. Somewhat mistakenly, as we shall shortly see, the mammalian Y chromosome is often said to be the sex determining chromosome, as if it determined *both* maleness and femaleness. More accurately, we can say that in most mammals the Y chromosome directs male development. In contrast, in birds, which also use a chromosomal rather than environmental mode of primary sex determination, females are the ones with the "different" chromosome, and female birds are said to be ZW while males are ZZ. Here too there is a male sex determining factor—this time on the Z chromosome. But flipping the switch to activate male development requires two doses of the Z factor thus ensuring that ZZ embryos become males and ZW embryos become females (Gilbert, 2010).

So far then, we have learned that a change in the social structure of a group of fishes or incubation temperature in reptiles can induce a sex change or produce extreme skewing of the ratio of males to females (the sex ratio). The fact that in these organisms the signal to differentiate one sex or the other does not emanate primarily from sex chromosomes does not contradict the idea that chromosomal make-up determines sex. Here the signals are physiological and to the extent that chromosomes are involved, signals might come from any chromosome, not just ones that carry specific genes for sexual development. But the environment of the mother or father can also sometimes change the ratio of male to female births in animals (e.g. birds and mammals) with chromosomal sex determination. Remember that both parents produce gametes (either a sperm or an egg) which carry autosomes plus a single sex chromosome. When sperm and egg fuse, two chromosomes (either both the same, or one of each different one) combine and the future is predictable. In theory the chances of producing either a male or a female is 50–50. In practice, "stuff happens."

If the truth be told, the number of males vs the number of females often deviates from 1:1. In rodents, some of the events leading to such deviations have been studied, but there is still a great deal of uncertainty about whether the results apply to humans (Cramer & Lumey, 2010; Kiely, Xu, McGeehin, Jackson, & Sinks, 1999; Rosenfeld & Roberts, 2004). For example, mice raised on rich diets produce litters with more males than females; fed on a poor diet, the sex ratio drops dramatically, with litters so skewed that there were three female pups for every one male born (Rivers & Crawford, 1974). In large mammals dominant females produce more males, and general stress before or during pregnancy leads to a decrease in sons (Rosenfeld & Roberts, 2004). Diet, dominance, and stress may all have similar downstream physiological effects on conception and pregnancy, so what may be at stake is a network that rebalances itself depending on environmental input thus skewing the sex ratio in one direction or the other.

While we do not know the specific mechanisms by which a mother produces more daughters or fewer sons, there are a number of logical possibilities:

1. post ejaculation the mother's physiological state could affect the motility and transport of X-bearing vs Y-bearing sperm, as they make their way towards the unfertilized egg. Or, there may be nutritional effects in the male that harm Y-bearing sperm development before ejaculation;
2. oocyte development might vary depending on the mother's physiological state, leading to the ovulation of an egg that fuses more easily with an X-bearing than a Y-bearing sperm;
3. an equal number of XX and XY embryos may start out in the uterus, but one type may grow better than the other. In the case of a low ratio of males to females, perhaps more of the XY embryos die very early in development.

No doubt there are other possible variations on the above themes. We are not close to understanding the mechanisms leading to a skewed sex ratio in animals with chromosomal sex determination. A couple of decades of dedicated research in this area would certainly bring greater clarity.

From Chromosomal Sex to Fetal Gonadal Sex

Words matter. The phrase "sex determination" suggests that one is talking about both male development *and* female development. But often in the scientific literature the term presages a discussion of male development only. For example, in many research papers the genetic factor on the mammalian Y chromosome is called the "sex determining factor" rather than the "male determining factor." When this elision occurs, the writer may say something to the effect that female development happens in the absence of a male-determining factor or may fail altogether to mention female development. Femaleness then becomes an absence, something that happens by default, something that does not merit the same level of scientific investigation as the more active male process.

There is a history here. Aristotle wrote "The female is a female by virtue of a lack of certain qualities" (Fausto-Sterling, 2000: 347). Much more recently, descriptions of the Oedipal drama (à la Freud) consider how the female psyche must accommodate to the absence of a penis, while the male must adjust to the fear of its loss and a return to some basal, default, female state. Given our rich past of conceptualizing the female as a lack or absence, it is probably more than an accident, although less than a conspiracy, that, when writing about sex determination, scientists slip without noticing into linguistic muddiness.

The cumulative result of this slippage has been a comparative lack of research on female development (Fausto-Sterling, 2000). Knowledge of ovarian development lags behind our understanding of the testis, a situation one group of scientists has called "amazing." Indeed, as have feminist critics since the 1980s (Fausto-Sterling, 1989), today's researchers acknowledge that one reason we still know comparatively little about the ovary is that "the prevailing view that ovarian development is the 'default' state [has] commonly led to an incorrect assumption that no active genetic steps need to be taken to specify or create an ovary," a view that is logically untenable given what we know about how genes act during development (Wilhelm, Palmer, & Koopman, 2007: 20). Slowly, but still very unevenly, scientists have begun to remedy this imbalance in knowledge about male vs female development and at the same time show that development and maintenance of the ovary does not rely on a passive molecular pathway (Veitia, 2010). A great example can be found in the work of Shoemaker and Crews (2009). Figure 3.1 is a simplified version of a diagram found on page 296 of their article.

Christina Shoemaker and David Crews, biologists at the University of Texas, Austin, divide vertebrate gonad development into two phases (Shoemaker & Crews, 2009). Initially, construction proceeds identically in chromosomally male and female embryos; the result is a pre-gonadal structure sometimes referred to as "equipotential" because it can develop in either a male or a female direction. In the older literature this undifferentiated gonad is called the "indifferent gonad."

In Figure 3.1 this point in the pathway comprises the base of the Y. A number of genetic factors act during this period, presumably as part

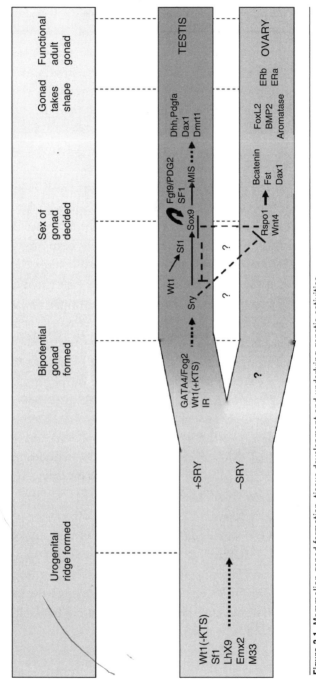

Figure 3.1 Mammalian gonad formation: tissue development and underlying genetic activities.

Note. Genetic events that underlie development of the gonad in mammals. Genes known to act at at specific developmental time points are listed. Solid lines indicate direct regulation of events. Dashed lines represent indirect or not yet completely defined relationships. The initials Wt1, SRY, GATA4, Fog2, KTS, IR, Sf1, Fgf9, PDG2, Mis, Sox9, Dhh, Pdgfa, Dax1, Dmrt1, Rspo1, Wnt4, Bcatenin, Fst, FoxL2, BMP2, ERb, ERa, each represent specific genes acting at the indicated location. Some of these are further explained in the text.

For a color version of this figure please go to www.routledge.com/cw/fausto-sterling

of equipotential gonad formation. And these factors act both in chromosomal male and chromosomal female embryos. (For linguistic simplicity I am writing as if everything always proceeds in the described manner. But of course any number of unexpected developments, such as a failure of one or more genes to act, or a genetic variant of some sort that acts in an unexpected manner, can alter the most frequent developmental pathways.)

Once the indifferent gonadal tissue forms, the gonad begins to develop in either a male or a female direction. For years scientists searched for the master gene that controls male development (sometimes erroneously called the master gene for sex determination). In mammals, the gene finally identified after a number of false starts is a male-determining factor on the Y chromosome called Sry (**S**ex **R**eversal on the **Y** chromosome). The product of the Sry gene binds to a control segment of a gene called Sox9 (**S**ry-related HMG **b**ox), which is located on the long arm of chromosome 17 (an autosome). Male development requires the actions of both Sry and Sox9 in the correct sequence and in the absence of either gene, potential males develop instead as females—with one exception: these women have no ovaries (Harley, Clarkson, & Argentaro, 2003). This points to the fact that a critical aspect of female sex determination—the steps that actively lead to ovary formation—is still poorly understood. As indicated in the diagram, several other genes participate in a reticulated pattern of gene activity directed at the formation of a normal testis. This is the process that sends *fetal gonadal sex* in a male direction. And it turns out the process runs more like a parliament than an autocratic director. It is time for new metaphors.

The indifferent gonad develops in a female direction under the influence of two genes (with, I suspect, more still to be discovered, since research here has lagged behind[2]). Both the gene **F**orkhead **b**ox protein **L**2 (FoxL2) and Wnt4 (**W**ingless type MMTV integration site family) control the activities of other genes in the ovarian differentiation gene network. FoxL2 resides on chromosome 3 and Wnt4 is on the 1st autosome. In mice missing FoxL2 and Wnt4 chromosomal females develop into males. In 2006 a new gene called **R-spo**ndin1 (Rspo1 found on autosome 1) emerged as a key player in female development. Both XX mice and XX humans lacking R-spondin1 activity develop testes and internal and external male genitalia even though they lack *Sry*, the so-called "master gene for male development" (Parma, Radi, Vidal, Chaboissier, Dellambra, Valentini, et al., 2006; Tomizuka, Horikoshi, Kitada, Sugawara, Iba, Kojima, et al., 2008).

Discovering the role of R-spondin1 in ovary development was a breakthrough in understanding the relationship between the developing male and female gonads. One current hypothesis is that Rspo1 and Wnt4 join forces to inhibit Sox9 activity and thus all of the testis differentiation factors that work downstream of Sox9. It now seems possible that Sry activity inhibits Rspo1, thus stopping female development. Cell biologists Leo DiNapoli and Blanche Capel note how the discovery of the role of R-spondin in ovary determination has changed how we frame our understanding of sex determination. Moving from the older representation of male development as active and female development as passive these scientists write, it seems that "the bipotential gonad is the battleground between two active and opposing signaling pathways . . ." (DiNapoli & Capel, 2008: 4).

So, with the help of these networks of clever molecules that signal cells to develop one way or the other, by the 12th week of human development human embryos have either actively developing testes or actively developing ovaries. *Fetal gonadal sex* (a.k.a. primary sex determination) is good to go. So good, in fact, that (at least the testes) take on developmental responsibilities by producing fetal gonadal sex hormones. *Fetal hormonal sex*, in turn, plays a critical role in the development of secondary sex determination—the differentiation of male or female internal organs and, in due time, the differentiation of the external genitalia.

From Fetal Hormonal Sex to Genital Sex

The theme of indifference, or bipotentiality, courses through the story of sexual development. Not only does the gonad itself begin as a bipotential structure, so too do the accessory ducts, needed to transport sperm or eggs, to sustain fetal development, and, generally, to carry out the nitty gritty of sexual reproduction. Hormones produced by the developing testes or ovaries select which set of ducts survive early development, and influence their proper differentiation.

In both XX and XY embryos, the bipotential gonad develops cheek by jowl with a structure called the mesonephros (literally, the middle kidney). In early mammalian development, the mesonephros functions as an embryonic kidney, but as development proceeds the emergence of the more familiar, bean-shaped kidneys (the metanephros) found at (and before) birth supplants the mesonephros' waste-elimination role. The middle kidneys connect via long ducts to a temporary embryonic structure called the cloaca.[3] While each XX and XY embryo has a pair of mesonephric kidneys and ducts to match the pair of gonads, the cloaca is a single centrally located structure (see Figure 3.2). But (as the overexcited TV ad man would yell) wait! There's more! Each XX and XY embryo, at this bipotential stage, sports another set of ducts that sit parallel to the mesonephric ducts, and like them, connect centrally to the cloaca. Because these lie right next to the mesonephric ducts, anatomists call them the paramesonephric ducts (also called the Müllerian ducts, after the anatomist who first found them).

From Fetal Gonadal Sex to Fetal Hormonal Sex and Thence (at last) to Genital Sex

Once the fetal gonads start to function, the double set of ducts begin to change. In humans, by about eight weeks, the fetal testis produces two critical hormones. The first, Anti-Müllerian Factor (AMF), eliminates the female developmental option by causing the paramesonephric ducts to degenerate. The second, fetal testosterone, repurposes the mesonephric ducts, influencing them to develop into the vas deferens, epididymis, and seminal vesicle. This early expression of *fetal hormonal sex* thus inhibits female development and encourages male differentiation. In XX embryos the fetal ovaries start to differentiate between eight and twelve weeks. Estrogen produced first by the mother and then by the fetal ovaries encourages the paramesonephric ducts to develop into the oviducts (Fallopian tubes), and where the tubes fuse along the anatomical midline, the uterus, cervix, and upper portion of the vagina form. As this female potential develops under the influence of *fetal hormonal sex*,

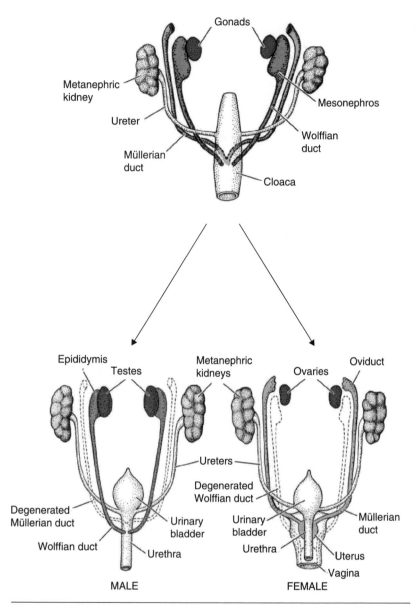

Figure 3.2 Development of male and female internal genital ducts.

For a color version of this figure please go to www.routledge.com/cw/fausto-sterling

the mesonephric ducts degenerate, possibly due to the absence of testosterone.

As the embryo establishes *internal reproductive sex* (all the aforementioned ducts and tubes), it starts, in an overlapping time dimension, to build *genital sex*. Here too, fetal hormonal sex plays a critical role. And here too, the fetus starts out indifferent, or bipotential, with regard to the external bits—penis, clitoris, scrotum, and vaginal folds (see Figure 3.3). In the moment of indifference both XX and XY infants have the identical phallus. The phallus, however, responds to fetal hormonal sex. Under the influence of androgens such as testosterone or dihydrotestosterone, it grows, differentiating into a penis. Under the influence of estrogen the phallus becomes a clitoris.

In analogous fashion, the labioscrotal swellings, identical at the bipotential stage, under the influence of androgen, fuse along the central midline to become the scrotum or they remain open to become the outer lips of the vagina. The urogenital folds either (when influenced by androgens) fuse along the midline, enclosing the urethra and becoming the shaft of the penis or remain open and become the inner lips of the vagina.[4] It should be noted that knowledge about the molecular details of external genital differentiation, including the precise role(s) of estrogen, remains underdeveloped. Here again, we know less about female than male development, and here as well, if researchers choose to investigate the details more thoroughly we will learn a great deal more than we currently understand. Nonetheless, at the end of this period during which external genital sex bifurcates from a bipotential anatomy to either male or female, we can say that the fetus has developed *genital sex*.

With all this bipotentiality going around, the fog surrounding the birth of infants with mixed sex may have begun to lift. All that needs to happen is that something out of the ordinary switches or derails the process of sexual development at one of the levels from chromosomal to genital sex. For example, rarely an XY child is conceived who carries a genetic mutation that prevents the body's cells from "seeing" or binding testosterone. Even though the fetal gonad produces androgens, the cells cannot capture the androgen molecules and thus cannot use them to move development in a male direction. Such androgen insensitive XY

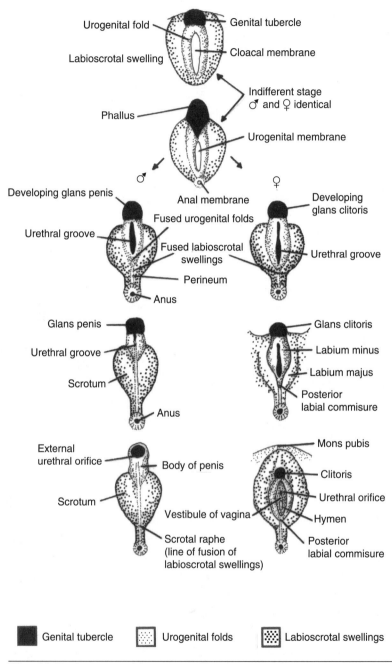

Figure 3.3 The development of the external genitalia from the indifferent (fetal) stage to full formation at birth.

Table 3.1 Some common types of intersexuality

Name	Cause	Basic clinical features
Congenital Adrenal Hyperplasia (CAH)	Genetically inherited malfunction of one or more of six enzymes involved in making steroid hormones	In XX children, can cause mild to severe masculinization of genitalia at birth or later; if untreated, can cause masculinization at puberty and early puberty. Some forms drastically disrupt salt metabolism and are life-threatening if not treated with cortisone.
Androgen Insensitivity Syndrome (AIS)	Genetically inherited change in the cell surface receptor for testosterone	XY children born with highly feminized genitalia. The body is "blind" to the presence of testosterone, since cells cannot capture it and use it to move development in a male direction. At puberty these children develop breasts and a feminine body shape.
Gonadal Dysgenesis	Various causes, not all genetic; a catch-all category	Refers to individuals (mostly XY) whose gonads do not develop properly. Clinical features are heterogeneous.
Hypospadias	Various causes, including alterations in testosterone metabolism	The urethra does not run to the tip of the penis. In mild forms, the opening is just shy of the tip; in moderate forms, it is along the shaft; and in severe forms, it may open at the base of the penis.
Turner Syndrome	Females lacking a second X chromosome (XO)	A form of gonadal dysgenesis in females. Ovaries do not develop; stature is short; lack of secondary sex characteristics; treatment includes estrogen and growth hormone.
Klinefelter Syndrome	Males with an extra X chromosome (XXY)	A form of gonadal dysgenesis causing infertility; after puberty there is often breast enlargement; treatments include testosterone therapy.

babies are born with highly feminized genitalia and are often identified as girls at birth, even though they are chromosomally and gonadally male. At puberty, still unable to respond to testosterone, they develop breasts and a feminine body shape by responding to the estrogen made by their testes. There are many other examples of intersexual development (now also called Disorders of Sexual Development, or DSDs), some of which I have listed in Table 3.1.

Finally, then, we have layered the more obvious bits and pieces of sex into a proper order of development and into their proper place. But we have yet to consider behavior and the brain—that astonishing organ that underpins our fears, our desires, our interests in particular types of partners, our emotions, our styles of courtship, etcetera, etcetera, etcetera. Does sex reach into the heart of our brains? Do brains have a sex? Read on.

Further Reading

Bagemihl, B. (1999). *Biological Exuberance: Animal Homosexuality and Natural Diversity.* New York: St. Martin's Press.

Capel, B. (2006). R-spondin1 tips the balance in sex determination. *Nature Genetics*, 38(11), 1233–1234.

Crews, David (1994). Animal sexuality. *Scientific American*, 270, 108–114.

Gilbert, S. F., & Epel, D. (2008). *Ecological Developmental Biology.* Sunderland, MA: Sinauer Associates.

Judson, Olivia (2003). *Dr. Tatiana's Sex Advice to All Creation: The Definitive Guide to the Evolutionary Biology of Sex.* New York: Holt Paperbacks.

Mason, R. T., & Crews, D. (1985). Female mimicry in garter snakes. *Nature*, 316(6023), 59–60.

4

OF HORMONES AND BRAINS

Do Brains Have a Sex?

Brain sex? John Money and Anke Ehrhardt proposed the idea decades ago. They drew the phrase from studies done on rats, birds, and the occasional primate. And the concept has had great staying power. Critics, myself included, have launched assaults on its edifice, but these have been repelled time after time. Today, if you let a computer search engine loose on the phrase, link after link turns up. There are books titled *Brain Sex*. There are self help guides to using knowledge about brain sex to advance one's career. There are theories of primary and secondary education based on the premise that boys and girls have different brains. And more—YouTube videos by the title, critiques of the idea, BBC nature films on the topic. You name it! You can probably find it.

The idea of brain sex has acquired a cultural valence and resonance that goes far beyond the scientific evidence that supports it. It is, in short, a meme,[1] which may explain why mere evidence cannot dislodge it from its secure castle. Ben Franklin is alleged to have said that: "One of the greatest tragedies in life is the murder of a beautiful theory by a gang of brutal facts." In the pages which follow we will explore the more scientific accounts of brain sex, evaluating what we do and do not know about the topic. Beware. You may witness a gang of brutal facts in action.

27

Brain Story I—The Genes (in Mice)

During the summer of 2010, in an article in the *New York Times*, science writer Nicholas Wade highlighted recent findings on gene activity in the (mouse) brain (Wade, 2010). At first blush, the story does not appear even to address the development of brain sex. That is, if what we mean by brain sex is the development of anatomical and functional brain differences in male and female fetuses, leading to sex-related differences in behavior after birth. But following the twists and turns of this complex story not only reveals some pretty interesting new science, it also demonstrates the memish nature of the idea of brain sex.

The story starts with Mom and Dad. During the process of producing either eggs or sperm, certain genes in each parent are temporarily modified. Modified genes are said to be *imprinted* by a chemical addition to the control element of the gene. This addition inactivates the gene during embryonic development. The process is called *epigenetic modification*. It is *epi* (over or above the gene) rather than actually genetic; i.e. it does not involve a genetic mutation, which would permanently alter the gene's structure. Sometimes imprinting suppresses the activity of a particular gene contributed by the mother but not the father. When this happens, the embryo must receive a good copy of the gene from the father in order to survive.[2] For other genes, the paternal contribution is suppressed and maternal gene expression predominates in the embryo (see Figure 4.1).

When this form of differential contribution from egg and sperm was first discovered, scientists thought that it applied to only a small number of genes. More recent findings in mice, however, show parentally biased gene expression for over 1,300 genes. For 347 of these genes, either the mother's or the father's copy was more actively expressed in particular regions of the developing brain (Gregg, Zhang, Butler, Haig, & Dulac, 2010). Even more intriguing is the finding that in the embryonic mouse brain, maternally contributed gene expression predominates, but in adult mice paternally contributed genes are preferentially active. Furthermore—and here the story gets a little dicey in terms of evidence, but also fascinating in terms of potential for future research revelations—the parental imprinting effects may work differently in the brains

Researchers have found that a surprising number of human genes are inherited asymmetrically, with one parent silencing genes that the other parent leaves active. The resulting genetic tug of war may explain why some genes are expressed differently in the brains of men and women.

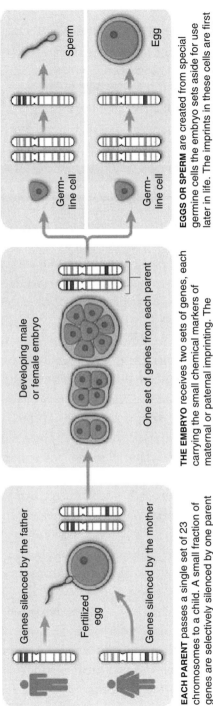

EACH PARENT passes a single set of 23 chromosomes to a child. A small fraction of genes are selectively silenced by one parent but not silenced by the other, in a genetic mechanism called imprinting.

THE EMBRYO receives two sets of genes, each carrying the small chemical markers of maternal or paternal imprinting. The developing embryo uses both genomes to construct its own body.

EGGS OR SPERM are created from special germine cells the embryo sets aside for use later in life. The imprints in these cells are first erased, then reapplied to match the sex of the embryo.

Genes silenced by the father

Genes silenced by the mother

Fertilized egg

Developing male or female embryo

One set of genes from each parent

Germ-line cell

Germ-line cell

Sperm

Egg

Figure 4.1 Mechanics of imprinting.

For a color version of this figure please go to www.routledge.com/cw/fausto-sterling

of sons and daughters (Gregg, Zhang, Weissbourd, Luo, Schroth, Haig, et al., 2010). The popular press presents these complex molecular events as a "tug of war" between parental genes. The *New York Times* quotes study's authors: "in your brain, your mom and your dad keep telling you what to do . . ." (Wade, 2010). While popularizers suggest that parents struggle to gain greater influence over their offspring, they also imply that in the end the conflict somehow produces different brains in male and female offspring. Here the chain of logic gets truly brittle. It is simply unclear how differential *parental* expression in all fetuses leads to different brain function in male vs female *fetal* brains and, in turn, to different patterns of male and female behavior. Nonetheless, this new work on parental imprinting and gene expression in the brain does something pretty important: it complicates a simpler, deeply entrenched story that fetal hormonal sex produces or causes brain sex differentiation.

Brain Story II—Hormones (Birds)

What *is* brain sex? Scientists use the term in three basic ways—measurable anatomy, brain physiology, and behavioral differences attributed to brain function. None of these are mutually exclusive. The most obvious is anatomy. For example, in humans, at the level of average differences between populations males have slightly larger brains than females. Such differences are not absolute: many men have smaller brains than many women, and vice versa. So while size is an example of a population-level sex difference, it can hardly count as brain sex—if we define the latter as something that differs between most men and most women. If overall size can't count as brain sex, what about differences in brain substructure? First, all males and all females have the same basic brain parts. However, some may be larger in males than in females, or vice versa.

Consider the canary. When not busy serving as an early warning system for coal miners, the male canary sings his heart out, using a song that female canaries don't sing at all. In a now classic study, behavioral biologists Fernando Nottebohm and Arthur Arnold (Nottebohm & Arnold, 1976) showed that the specific region of the canary brain responsible for the male song was strikingly larger in males than females. Furthermore, when they injected females with testosterone, their song specific region grew and the girls started to sing a version of the missing song. Here, then, is direct evidence of something we can call brain sex: usually male and female canaries have a large anatomical (size/neuron number) difference in a specific region of the brain; the difference can be linked to a specific function and high concentrations of a sex-differentiated hormone. Furthermore, when the sex that lacks the hormone receives it via injection, the cells in the specific location increase in number under the influence of a hormone, and a specific sex-differentiated function appears.

But life, and especially natural diversity, is rarely consistent or simple. For canaries and a number of other songbirds, more brain "hardware" correlates with more singing. Structure precedes function. But the same cannot be said for all birds. For example, African forest weaver birds have clear male–female anatomical differences in specific "song control" regions of the brain. Yet, males and females sing almost identical songs, usually in loving unison. This brain sex story is far from a simple equation between structure and function.

Male and female forest weaver mates sing in unison. Given the earlier work on canaries, scientists predicted that their brain anatomy in the crucial areas responsible for song production would be identical. But, when they looked (remember that gang of facts, assaulting the beautiful theory), they found that for both volume and number of neurons, males had more than 1.5 times larger structures than females. However, when they examined the levels of gene expression for several genes known for their specialized activity in vocalization areas of the brain, they found what amounts to an inverse image of the anatomical differences: while the male brain regions for singing were larger and had more cells, song-crucial gene activity in the female was much greater than in the male. In effect the gene action advantage canceled out the size advantage leading to equal song production abilities (Gahr, Metzdorf, Schmidl, & Wickler, 2008; Gahr, Sonnenschein, & Wickler, 1998).

This seems pretty messy. Why not just have equally sized brain structures for equally performed functions? We don't know for sure, but researchers have suggested some hypotheses that depend on the forest weavers' evolutionary history. What if, for example, the forest weavers descended from ancestors that were more like canaries in terms of song patterns? That is, the males sang and the females didn't. In these ancestors, a canary-style pattern of brain structure existed. Perhaps due to small natural variations in testosterone production, female singing started to evolve and duet-facilitated pairing slowly resulted; if there were strong reproductive advantages to couples in which both sexes sang together (birds that sing together swing together?), how might females ramp up their singing capacity? Natural selection for ever-increasing testosterone levels probably wouldn't have worked. First, in canaries long periods of high testosterone actually start to inhibit vocal development. Second, long periods of elevated testosterone would probably interfere with female reproductive abilities. So how else could selection for increased female singing act? Plausibly, by favoring increased activity levels for critical genes involved in song production. This would involve increased frequencies of subtle mutations in the population, or epigenetic changes at the gene regulatory sites governing the critically acting genes. In short, there is more than one way to get a bird to sing. Future research will certainly test this and other hypotheses, so stay tuned.

Brain Story III—The Rodents

As with humans, when the bipotential gonad transforms into a testis in XY rodents, it starts to pump out testosterone. In rodents we know that this hormone makes its way to the brain, and that in some parts of the brain, enzymes convert it to estrogen. The estrogen, in turn, has proven developmental effects on two regions of the brain—small centers within the hypothalamus, and the preoptic area (see Figure 4.2). These two regions are critical sites for regulation of physiological functions related specifically to reproduction—i.e. regulation of the patterns of testis function vs ovarian development and cyclical ovulation, and of hormonal regulation of pregnancy, delivery, and lactation. So far so good, and not too surprising.

In the late 1950s a germinal paper appeared that expanded the concept that fetal hormones affected the development of reproductive physiology,

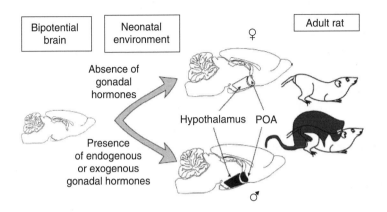

Figure 4.2 Classic model of the organizational and activational effects of steroids on development: reproduction parameters.

to the more general idea that fetal hormones "organized" brain development in ways that might affect a wide variety of sex-differentiated behaviors (Fausto-Sterling, 2000; McCarthy & Konkle, 2005). The specific studies, performed on guinea pigs (I know, they are not technically rodents, but get thrown into the rodent basket to simplify discussion), examined mounting behavior (in males) and receptive back-arching (lordosis) in females; thus this most conclusive evidence of prenatal brain organization extended still to only very specific behaviors related to reproduction. Since 1959 a very large number of studies have invoked the idea that prenatal hormones organize the fetal brain (i.e. produce *brain sex*) and that such fetal "organization" forms the basis for a wide variety of different behaviors and abilities. This includes claims that human (and rodent) males and females have different mental abilities because they were exposed to different hormonal cocktails *in utero*.

While in the ensuing 50 odd years we have learned an enormous amount about the cellular and molecular mechanisms by which hormones affect nervous tissue development (Morris, Jordan, & Breedlove, 2004; Simerly, 2002), evidence that these hormones produce specific brain changes related to non-reproductive behaviors, even in rodents, remains weak (Fine, 2010; Jordan-Young, 2010; McCarthy & Konkle, 2005; Morris et al., 2004). Two University of Maryland-based neuroscientists, M. M. McCarthy, and A. T. Konkle (2005) argue forcefully that "there has been an increasing tendency to equate 'sex differences' with 'sex dimorphisms'." By "dimorphism," they mean large differences that have little overlap (e.g. the difference in the song region of the brain in male and female canaries), be they behavioral or anatomical. The more commonly used phrase "sex difference," however, refers to small average differences between two groups, with considerable overlap (e.g. the differences found between males and females on language ability performances on college test scores). (As an illustration, we can think of a dimorphism as being analogous to the difference in size between a chihuahua and a Saint Bernard (see Figure 4.3). Not much

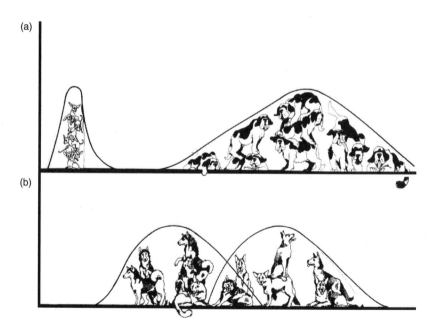

Source: Alyce Santoro for the author.

Figure 4.3 (a) Comparing chihuahuas to Saint Bernards. (b) Comparing huskies to German shepherds.

overlap in size there. On the other hand, German shepherds are on average somewhat larger than huskies, but there is quite a bit of size overlap.) While there are well established examples in rodents and birds of brain sex dimorphisms, the strong cases all have something to do with reproduction—the one place where we might expect it. But still, if not rodents, then maybe primates show brain sex that governs a wide variety of non-reproductive behaviors.

Some "older work," that is work that is well known and has been in the literature for a good 20 years, illustrates certain of the conceptual problems we face in trying to pinpoint sex differences in neural tissue that function in the cognitive or sensory parts of the brain rather than being primary in reproductive function. There are lots of studies of sex differences in the brains of lab rats. In most cases the rats are raised to be general issue. After they are weaned they are isolated in wire cages and all fed and watered alike. There is not much to do in those cages. But what happens if they are raised in an enriched environment? (Think how different the experience of a wild rat must be.)

In the 1980s experimental psychologist Janice Juraska started comparing the brains of rats raised in the standard isolated way (IC=Isolated Condition) with those raised in an enriched environment (EC=Environmentally Complex). Once weaned, these latter rats got to live in a group home with about a dozen rats of the same sex. Not only that, every day Juraska removed the previous day's toys and put in different ones. Then she compared anatomical differences in the nerve cells of males and females raised under either the IC or EC conditions. She specifically looked at non-reproductive areas of the brain—the cerebral cortex, and the corpus callosum. Since the general take home message—environment affects sex differences—was the same for each brain region we only need to see her results for the hippocampus to get the big lesson (Juraska, 1991).

The hippocampus plays an important role in spatial navigation and long term memory and has been invoked to explain alleged differences in spatial ability in rodents and in humans. (I say "alleged" because there is disagreement about the existence or at least the origins of such differences.) Juraska took rats at weaning and housed them in either EC or

IC environments for a month, until they reached puberty. She then measured the degree of branching of individual hippocampal neurons. The degree of branching provided a measure of how well connected each neuron was with other neurons. In the IC conditions there was a clear sex difference: neurons from males were more highly branched than ones from females. The differences were of the husky–German shepherd size, 1.1 to 1.2 times as much branching in the (IC) male compared to the (IC) female brains.

When Juraska compared the hippocampus of EC rats there was a similar sized sex difference, but with a surprising twist. This time the females had more highly branched neurons than the males! Will the real sex difference please stand up? Well, of course, both sex differences are real, but they only apply to the environment in which the rats grew up. The lesson, then, for these studies of sex differences in the anatomy of non-reproductive brain regions is twofold. First, the size of the differences is considerably smaller than differences found in brain regions governing reproduction. Second, the direction of difference changes dramatically depending on the rearing environment.

Juraska also wondered whether and how hormones might be involved in producing the sex differences. She found that for the males, testosterone probably suppresses the ability of their hippocampal neurons to respond to the enriched environment. The possible role of estrogen in the neuronal branching is less clear and she concludes that we are still far from understanding the role of hormones in the sexual differentiation of this and other regions of the brain.

Brain Story IV—Humans

Sex-related development in the rodent nervous system depends on particular mixes of hormone, age, strain and species, maternal attention, and rearing environment. Is this also true for humans? In rodents, no matter how complex the story is, scientists conduct controlled experiments. They manipulate variables, removing gonads, adding in hormones; they raise animals in impoverished or enriched environments and cross foster pups between anxious or calm mothers. Because we have high ethical standards for the conduct of research on human subjects, however, none of this can we willfully do in humans. Instead we resort to so-called "quasi-experiments." In a true experiment investigating the effects of prenatal hormones on human brain development, scientists would randomly assign subjects to receive particular hormone exposures and would follow their development over a lifetime. Since this would be unethical, scientists instead rely on less robust evidence. They stitch together information from developmental accidents—hormonal exposures due to medicines ingested during pregnancy and the like.

In a quasi-experiment much is unknown. Usually we do not know the dose of hormone exposure, nor its exact timing and duration. In humans, genital and reproductive structures develop fairly quickly and early in fetal development. The human brain, however, develops slowly but continuously throughout fetal development. The baby arrives with some basic shelving—the parts of the brain (cerebrum, cerebellum, etc.) are fleshed out and there are many nerve cells (neurons). But the nerve cells still need a lot of refinement. For one thing—relative to a 5 year old—they are poorly connected. After birth, and for the next five years the human brain triples or quadruples in size, mostly because those cells already present at birth become more and more complex and interconnected.

Here's one example: nerve cells (neurons) use specialized structures called synapses to transmit signals to one another. The more synapses in a given space, the more information can pass back and forth and the more complex the transmission networks. In human newborns many parts of the brain start off with a small density of synapses. By 3 months synapse density doubles, and by 3.3 years it peaks at three times the starting density (Figure 4.4). Another way to look at the development of cells in the brain is to measure how bushy individual neurons get. This bushiness develops as individual cells branch to form more and more cell connections (via those aforementioned synapses). Again, the more prolific the branching, the greater the complexity of the nervous system and the more complex an infant's possible behaviors. In newborns individual nerve cells are pretty straight. By adulthood there is an exuberance of branches—as much as 800 times more than at birth.

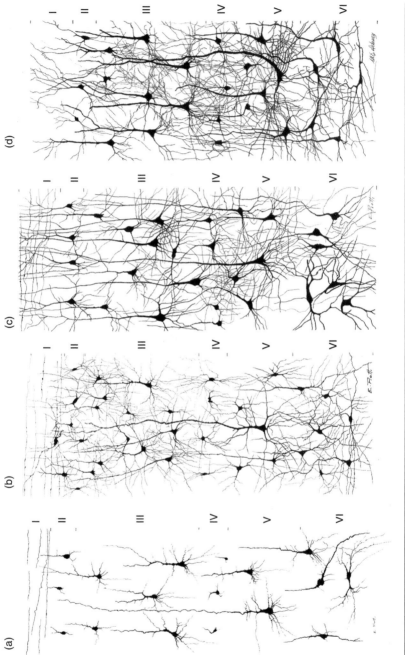

Figure 4.4 Drawings of the nerve cells and their connections in the fusiform gyrus of the cerebral cortex at birth, 3, 6, and 15 months. This region of the brain is involved in processing color information, face and body recognition, word recognition, and within-category identification.

With increased synapsing and branching comes enormous possibility. Consider the improvement in vision, the development of motor skills (walking, holding a fork and eating, threading a needle), language, and all sorts of independent behaviors that emerge as an infant grows from total dependency into self sufficiency, and then imagine the elaboration of behavioral masculinity and femininity in this same developmental context.

What, then, can a quasi-experiment tell us about prenatal hormones and possible sex differences in brain structure or function? Consider the many studies of girls born with a genetic anomaly called Cortical Adrenal Hyperplasia (CAH). Due to an enzyme malfunction, the adrenals of CAH girls make unusually large amounts of androgen, starting midway through fetal development. Even though these girls have ovaries, the adrenal androgens masculinize their genitals, sometimes to such a degree that these XX infants with fully female internal plumbing can be mistaken for boys at birth. The adrenal malfunction, however, leads to an acute medical crisis, and in the ensuing medical response even the highly male-appearing XX babies are identified as girls. Once so labeled, they receive hormone treatment that reduces the high androgen levels. Usually they also undergo genital surgery to make their genitals appear more female-like (Fausto-Sterling, 2000).

Here is the quasi-experiment. Most likely, adrenal testosterone traveled through the fetal circulatory system, thus exposing the developing fetal brain to unusually high levels of testosterone, although we don't know exactly how high the exposure was or when it began and even if it was continuous once it started. We also know that due to medical intervention high testosterone exposure stopped shortly after birth, that at first there was some confusion about the sex of the infant, and that there was considerable medical attention including ongoing hormonal medication and usually genital surgery all in the first 1–2 years of life. The question: does the early exposure to high levels of androgen affect the play behavior of these children, and can we attribute any differences to the effects of prenatal testosterone on the brain?

And the answer (drum roll please, wait while I open the envelope . . .) is—sort of, maybe, possibly? Play, of course, involves several behaviors including general energy expenditure, and the types of toys or games as well as the playmates a child chooses. A perusal of 18 studies of play behavior in CAH girls at first looks very impressive. Fourteen of them report more masculine behavior in the CAH girls compared to controls. (Controls are often unaffected sisters.) However, the results become more confusing when divided up by domain. For example, CAH girls do not particularly prefer playing with boys (compared to controls) (Berenbaum & Snyder, 1995; Jordan-Young, 2010). Researchers have also come up empty-handed when looking for activity differences between CAH and normal girls. For example, when psychologist Melissa Hines and her co-workers observed sex differences in what is commonly call rough and tumble play (school-age boys do more of it than girls), they found no differences between CAH girls and unaffected controls (Hines & Kaufman, 1994). Finally, despite some early reports, there do not seem to be any reliable differences in dominance, high energy play, and assertiveness between CAH girls and unaffected controls (Dittman, Kappes, Kappes, Börger, Willig, & Wallis, 1990). The one consistent finding has been that CAH girls prefer more masculine toys (trucks and blocks) than controls and are a bit less likely to play with feminine toys such as dolls or cooking implements (Hines, 2009; Jordan-Young, 2010).

So, of all the play behaviors examined, toy choice correlates with CAH in girls. Is this good evidence that androgen overproduction *in utero* is the cause? Again, let's return to the nature of the quasi-experiment. If these were rats, experimenters could "sacrifice" them at the end of the experiments and examine their brains. But these are children, beloved of their parents, with all of the human rights society affords. So no peeking at the brain. Instead, researchers try to imagine the possible causes of the correlation and then argue for or against each possibility. The last cause standing, as it were, is designated as the real cause. This is where all the arguing starts. And not only will it not end, it can't end, unless in the future we find a clear, non-invasive way to study the fine details of brain anatomy and physiology on living humans.

But let's get a flavor of the possibilities, as so beautifully proposed and elaborated by Rebecca Jordan-Young (2010).

Attitude 1: Prenatal hormones produce sex differences in the brain. Many scientists find this to be the most economical explanation. There are several counter arguments, however. For example, since other hormones (e.g. cortisone) are also disrupted in fetuses with CAH, perhaps it is not testosterone per se but some other aspect of the disease that contributes to the altered toy preference. Or, maybe the hormone effects are indirect, i.e. they don't change the brain but some other aspect of development such as motor skills or temperament.

Attitude 2: The correlation of toy preference and CAH results from social responses to the developmental disorder. Proponents of the prenatal hormone explanation have tried to assess whether parents behave differently to CAH girls than to unaffected sisters. The measures used in such assessments either involve retrospective questionnaires or direct observations in which the observers know which children are CAH and which are not. Each of these approaches is flawed, either by relying on memory of events in which the parents have a heavy emotional investment, or by making observations without a blind or double blind experimental structure. Some proponents of Attitude 2 suggest that the fact that CAH girls have been under intense medical treatment and have possibly had early genital surgery has in some way affected the development of toy preference (Kessler, 1998). To assess this possibility other types of control comparisons would need to be made.

Attitude 3: Prenatal hormones influence the development of certain traits, but they are far from the sole or direct cause. One study (not a quasi-experiment, but a correlational experiment studying normal role variability) reported a correlation between more masculine gender role development in girls and maternal testosterone measured during pregnancy. But the correlation accounted for only 2 percent of the variability in gender role behaviors for the girls they studied. Although the authors emphasize the importance of the relationship, they also point out both that it is small, and not necessarily causal or due to a direct effect on brain development (Hines, Golombok, Rust, Johnston, & Golding, 2002).

The point is that quasi-experiments (and there are many more; the CAH example is just one example) provide informative data. They are worth doing because they represent one of only a few sources of information specifically derived from human development. But by their very nature, the interpretation of results from quasi-experiments remains open to ongoing debate (Fine, 2010). One recent scientific review summed up the difficulty: "The complexity of human behavior, which is powerfully shaped by social influences, makes it difficult to answer " the question of whether prenatal testosterone accounts for behavioral differences between men and women (Morris et al., 2004: 1038). But we do know that at birth the surrounding adults use external genital sex to identify new babies as boys or girls. And, according to John Money's developmental story, it is this knowledge (possibly combined with effects of prenatal hormones) that leads to the next step—the development of gender identity.

Further Reading

Hines, M. (2005). *Brain Gender*. Oxford: Oxford University Press.

Jordan-Young, R. M. (2010). *Brainstorm: The Flaws in the Science of Sex Differences*. Cambridge, MA: Harvard University Press.

Schulkin, J. (2004). *Bodily Sensibility: Intelligent Action*. Oxford: Oxford University Press.

To watch a great set of videos on the normal development of the human brain, you can access and explore the following website: http://changingbrains.org.

5

AM I A BOY OR A GIRL?—THE EMERGENCE OF GENDER IDENTITY

Learning from Quasi-Experiments

In their early work, Money and colleagues treated gender identity as if it formed without biological influence. By 1972, in their classic book *Man and Woman, Boy and Girl*, Money and his colleague Anke Ehrhardt were less certain of the idea of total plasticity, but still emphasized the high degree of malleability in gender identity formation in the first two years of life (Money & Ehrhardt, 1972). Regardless of what combination of biological and social forces contributed to gender identity formation, Money and Ehrhardt believed that gender identity became fixed at some point around 2 years of age. Their concept of early identity fixation became the underpinning for the view that "corrective" surgery for children born with ambiguous genitalia needed to be done swiftly. In more recent years, many have criticized the practice of early surgery (Dreger, 1998a, 1998b; Fausto-Sterling, 2000; Kessler, 1998).

Money's beliefs about the social influences on gender identity formation held remarkable sway for several decades. One scientist who consistently challenged his point of view was Milton Diamond. He emphasized the idea that fetal gonadal hormones influenced the fetal brain to produce "brain sex"; for Diamond (and others) fetal hormonal sex not only led to different interests in boys and girls (see discussion in Chapter 4), even more profoundly, fetal hormones preconditioned the brain so that under most circumstances gender identity itself formed consistently with all of the previous events of sexual development (Diamond, 1965). The most extreme statement of this point of view eliminates altogether the role of gender reinforcement from surrounding adults or of forming body image. Some scientists believe that the correct brain sex alone, formed before birth, leads to proper gender identity formation. As development proceeds into the postnatal period, the child starts to manifest his or her gender identity.

For decades Diamond could not obtain a wide hearing for his ideas, but all that changed when (due to Diamond's efforts) it became clear that Money had cooked the books on one of his key pieces of evidence— the claim that a normally formed XY boy had been successfully transformed into a girl with a female gender identity following reconstructive surgery and careful instructions to the parents to rear "him" as a girl. (This unlikely process was necessitated by a botched circumcision that destroyed the infant boy's penis (Colapinto, 2001; Diamond & Sigmundson, 1997; Fausto-Sterling, 2000).) This is, of course, the famous Joan/John case, filled with personal tragedy and high drama and sensationalized in popular books (Colapinto, 2001).

John Money's downfall ushered in an almost complete swing of the nature–nurture pendulum. Claims of biological determination of gender identity formation ascended while the idea that socialization contributed importantly to gender identity formation became subject to ridicule. How, then, does the evidence stack up today? In their prescient 1978 book, Kessler and McKenna developed a table to assess the relationship between often-accepted biological factors and the development of gender. Here I acknowledge their influence as I redraw the table to focus on gender identity and incorporate more recent biological and medical findings (Table 5.1).

First, Money was right that chromosomal sex, gonadal sex, internal reproductive organs, external genitalia, and pubertal hormones are not direct determinants of gender identity. The extensive study of individuals for whom gender identity and one or more of these biological formations is discordant makes this quite clear. Thus, most XY individuals (who also have testes) who are completely insensitive to their

Table 5.1 Biological factors and gender identity development: what do we know?

Biologists' criteria for gender I.D. determination	Relationship	Evidence from quasi-experiments
Chromosomes	No	Androgen insensitivity syndrome
Gonads	No	Turner syndrome
Internal reproductive organs	No	Turner syndrome
Prenatal hormones	Possible	No direct evidence
External genitalia	No	Transsexuals
Pubertal hormones	No	CAH assigned as male at birth
Other	Under debate	Cloacal exstrophy
		Childhood gender identity disorder
		Adult transsexual narratives
		Brain studies of adult transsexuals
		Finger length ratios

own androgens develop a female gender identity (androgen insensitivity, in Table 5.1). Similarly, in extreme cases of congenital adrenal hyperplasia (androgen overproduction *in utero*) XX individuals may develop a male gender identity despite having ovaries and a uterus. The idea that prenatal hormones affect brain development in some manner that influences gender identity formation remains a favorite hypothesis despite a lack of direct evidence or the elucidation of a specific developmental pathway to support it.

In the absence of direct evidence the prenatal hormone hypothesis takes the following form: the fetal gonad produces hormones that affect brain development in some unspecified manner. The assumption is that the brain produces gender identity. In the most extreme version, there are no social influences on brain identity development. On other renderings, the hormones are understood to "predispose" the brain to develop a particular gender identity, although what the nature of such a predisposition might be is unclear. Those who believe strongly in a hormone-brain-identity nexus have quasi-experiments to support their case. Here we examine two of these—the study of gender assignment and acceptance in children born with various disorders of sexual development and the study of childhood gender dysphoria.

Psychologist Melissa Hines and her colleagues studied the gender identity of adult women and men with congenital adrenal hyperplasia. Unaffected male or female relatives served as controls. The study subjects filled out questionnaires that asked them to remember what kinds of toys they played with during childhood, what their adult love lives and fantasies consisted of, and how satisfied they were living as males or females. We will focus on the last of these questions. In psychology you are what you measure. Professor Hines and her colleagues measured core gender identity by asking the questions listed in Table 5.2. There are three distinct aspects of their query: do their subjects enjoy being a person of his or her own sex, do they wish they were the other sex, and do they psychologically believe they *are* the other sex? (Hines, Brook, & Conway, 2004).

Table 5.2 Questionnaire on core gender identity

Answer "always, almost always, most of the time, about half, only some, almost never, never" to indicate the degree to which you agree or disagree with the following statements:

1. During the *past 12 months*, my behavior has been what most people in this country consider appropriate for my sex;

2. During my *lifetime*, my behavior has been what most people in this country consider appropriate for my sex;

3. During the *past 12 months*, I have enjoyed being a person of my sex;

4. During my *lifetime*, I have enjoyed being a person of my sex;

5. During the *past 12 months*, I have wished I were a person of the opposite sex;

6. During my *lifetime*, I have wished I were a person of the opposite sex;

7. During the *past 12 months*, I have thought I was psychologically a person of the opposite sex;

8. During my *lifetime*, I have thought I was psychologically a person of the opposite sex.

During the year preceding the administration of the questionnaire, CAH women scored significantly higher (i.e. less satisfied) on the three types of gender identity questions than did the control women. Two things about this. First, the difference was large but overlapped by about 57 percent. Second, to measure Gender Identity Disorder (GID) they lumped together different types of questions, even though the questions are not all equally about gender identity. The last question is the most focused on actual identity, i.e. believing oneself to be a male. The first might be understood to focus on happiness with gender roles (as opposed to identity) and the second could be a response to perceived advantages of being male rather than female. Taken together, Hines and colleagues conclude that "women with CAH reported weaker identification as females." (Hines et al., 2004: 78). Since, however, we don't know the results of each of the separate questions, it remains unclear whether this means that early androgen exposure masculinized gender identity—the sense of oneself as female—or merely increased dissatisfaction with a more feminine role. The results of this quasi-experiment are suggestive, but not conclusive. Does fetal androgen exposure "set" later gender identity? Probably not definitively, or all the CAH women would believe themselves to be men. Does early testosterone exposure influence later gender identity formation? Possibly, via pathways that are likely to be indirect.

In addition to the study of CAH women, three rare conditions, cloacal exstrophy of the bladder, penile agenesis (failure of the penis to develop), and traumatic loss of the penis at a very young age (Meyer-Bahlburg, 2005) provide us with information about the development of gender identity. Cloacal exstrophy is a rare birth defect in which infants are born without external genitalia and with other malformations of the bladder and surrounding tissue. This used to be a lethal condition, but in recent years surgeons have successfully reconstructed such children, usually shaping them as females. For 46 XY patients this has meant surgical feminization, removal of the testes, and assigning the infants as females. So here is the quasi-experiment. How successful have these female reassignments of XY infants who *probably* developed with male prenatal hormonal sex been? The assumption is that these XY children were exposed to androgens prenatally but since we don't know what caused the cloacal exstrophy, we can't be sure that this assumption is correct. Still, the logic for this quasi-experiment is: if fetal hormonal exposure determines gender identity, then assigning these XY infants to be raised as girls should not work. If other factors (social and/or biological) contribute importantly to gender identity formation, then such children can succeed in developing a female gender identity.

Meyer-Bahlburg reviewed the cases of XY children with cloacal exstrophy who had been assigned and raised as either girls or boys. Of 51 patients with early female gender assignment, 33 were still living as females, 11 were living as males, and seven had expressed wishes to become male. Male-assigned and raised patients (279 to date) all were still living as males at the time of publication. One was starting to express a desire to become female. Many of these patients are still young, and their choices may well change as they progress through adulthood (Meyer-Bahlburg, 2005).

An update by Dr. William Reiner, the researcher whose work Meyer-Bahlburg cites, contains the following information: in his series of 60 people (two of whom died at aged 16): 60 percent have transitioned to male and 40 percent remain female (Reiner, 2010: personal communication). Three remain homebound with their parents due to health issues and one of these transitioned to male spontaneously at age 18, one tried to transition at age 9 but was rebuffed by her parents, and one who was told her medical history at age 12 years, now about 20, remains female. Only four of the other remaining females know anything about their genetics or birth history. Some of the reasons the adults gave for transitioning was that it made sense to them (#1), that they fit in better by transitioning (#2), and that it was easier to approach girls (women) as a male, which they identified with anyway—and that apparently turned out to be true (the ease of approaching, that is).

One result from Reiner's studies is especially worth noting. In all of his cases of XY children born with cloacal dystrophy—those who remained as women as well as those who chose to become males—none have expressed sexual attraction to other males. We don't know enough about the possible *in utero* causes of cloacal dystrophy to offer serious hypotheses about why this might be so. But for this group of 60 people, being chromosomally male seems strongly linked to a later expression of male heterosexual desire. As the future study of gender identity and sexual orientation unfolds, this factoid is worth keeping in mind. The sample sizes for cases with penile agenesis or traumatic loss are small. But when Meyer-Bahlburg adds these results to the cloacal exstrophy studies, the following picture emerges: 69 percent of the female-assigned XY children of childhood age (including 7 percent who expressed desires to change sex) lived as females; 91 percent of the adolescent aged children (including 23 percent who wished to change sex) lived as females; in adulthood fewer—65 percent (including 18 percent who wished to transition to male) lived as women. By contrast all XY patients, in all age groups, who were assigned and raised as males, chose to remain male. Meyer-Bahlburg concludes that the data do not indicate full biological determination of gender identity, either by prenatal hormones or genetic or other factors. He concludes that "gender assignment and the concomitant social factors have a major influence on gender outcome" (Meyer-Bahlburg, 2005: 432).

Learning from Developmental Psychology

If Meyer-Bahlburg is right, then looking at postnatal development can teach us a lot about gender identity formation. Our first clues come from a simple timeline, constructed by developmental psychologists over years of careful study and clever experimentation. Consider the information presented in Figures 5.1 and 5.2. Figure 5.1a emphasizes both the overlapping differences observed in boys and girls at birth and the fact that in these first postnatal months, development depends on the primary caregiver—most often the mother. The unit of interest is the mother–infant dyad rather than the individual. And we see that mothers often communicate more with girls in face to face interactions and intersect more physically with boys. The dyad guides the development of the infant, so that by 6 months some report that girls look

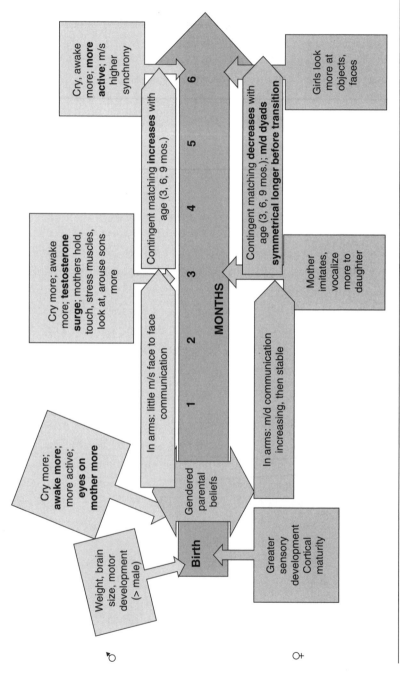

Figure 5.1 Developmental timelines. (a) Sex/gender from birth to 6 months.

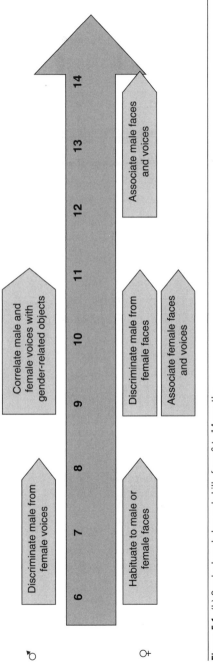

Figure 5.1 (b) Gender knowledge and skills from 6 to 14 months.

For a color version of this figure please go to www.routledge.com/cw/fausto-sterling

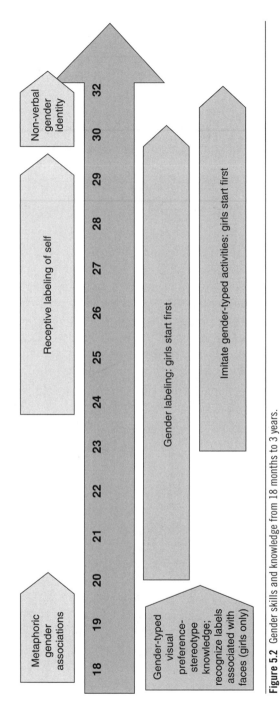

Figure 5.2 Gender skills and knowledge from 18 months to 3 years.

For a color version of this figure please go to www.routledge.com/cw/fausto-sterling

more at objects and faces than boys (Fausto-Sterling, García Coll, & Lamarre, 2011a, 2011b). As we consider this gender timeline I need to emphasize its limitations. The most important of these is that the information we have comes overwhelmingly from studies done in the United States and Western Europe. While cultural variability, of course, exists in this setting, it may be small compared to many other cultures worldwide. For this reason, the timeline and discussion I develop here ought not to be taken as universal, i.e. applying timelessly and without geographical restriction to all humans. Indeed, one of the virtues of developing a dynamic and developmental approach to understanding human development is that we can devise general principles of study that still require historical and cultural specificity.

It doesn't take long for babies to discern gender in their environment. By as early as 3–4 months infants can tell the difference between male and female voices, and seem to recognize the difference between male and female faces as well (Quinn, Yahr, Kuhn, Slater, & Pascalils, 2002). How do we know this? Since such young infants can't tell us what they see, we infer it by carefully watching how their eyes fix on a subject. First experimenters showed infants slides of different women in different clothing and with different hairstyles. After a while the infant does not fixate for long on a new female slide. However, when slides of men are added in, the infants recognize that there is something new in the mix and stare longer at them.

Infants start their journey into gender knowledge by learning to distinguish between adult male and adult female voices and to recognize that men and women look different. In the second half of year one these skills become a bit more sophisticated. In addition to habituating to female faces, they can habituate to male faces and can associate female faces with female voices. This latter skill is what psychologists call "intermodal" association, that is the infant can combine and interpret the hearing mode and the visual mode together to produce richer information about gender (Poulin-Dubois, Serbin, & Derbyshire, 1998). The gender-related skill of associating male voices and faces seems to develop a bit later, by about 1 year of age (Martin, Ruble, & Szkrybalo, 2002;

Ruble, Martin, & Berenbaum, 2006). Finally, by 10 months infants have begun to acquire some of the cognitive skills needed to create gender categories. For example, in an artificial testing situation 10 month olds can associate pictures of males and females with male and female voices (Poulin-Dubois, Serbin, Kenyon, & Derbyshire, 1994). They can also create categories in which they associate pictures of males with items such as hammers and footballs, and pictures of females with items such as a scarf or a frying pan (Levy & Haaf, 1994). This means that even before the age of one, infants have assimilated the gendered connections that surround them.

As children enter their second year (Figure 5.2) they add complex skills such as metaphorically linking neutral items with one or the other sex. For example, in one study 18 month to 2 year olds identified fire hats, hammers, fir trees, and bears with males (Eichstedt, Serbin, Poulin-Dubois, & Sen, 2002). In this same time period boys preferred to look at trucks and girls at dolls, a fascinating contrast to results from 12 month olds, where both boys and girls preferred to look at dolls. Despite these visual preferences, even at 2 years of age neither boys nor girls associated gender-stereotyped toys with photos of faces of children of a specific sex (Serbin, Poulin-Dubois, Colburne, Sen, & Eichstedt, 2001).

As they enter their third year children's knowledge of culturally specific gender picks up steam, and kids start to express self awareness of themselves as boys or girls. In other words, gender identity emerges. It does not suddenly pop out; rather it inches into the open—one step at a time. First, infants develop receptive labeling: he or she can correctly answer the question, "Are you a boy or a girl?" (Martin et al., 2002). This is called receptive labeling. Then they become aware of "gender appropriate" activities and can imitate them using toys such as dolls or toy vacuum cleaners (Poulin-Dubois, Serbin, Eichstedt, Sen, & Beissel, 2002). For example, they stare longer if shown a picture of a man putting on lipstick or a woman with a hammer (Serbin, Poulin-Dubois, & Eichstedt, 2002). Generally, girls seem to learn these stereotyped activities a few months before boys, but by 3 years both sexes are pretty conversant with culturally specific gender stereotypes and they can actively label themselves as either a boy or a girl (Weinraub, Clemens, Sockloff, Ethridge, Gracely, & Myers, 1984).

To sum up: children first develop sex and gender knowledge including the sensory and cognitive skills to make culturally "correct" associations between adult activities and males and females. They also develop culturally "correct" play preferences, and as they master these skills they place themselves in the gender picture, learning first to accept a label of male or female and then to self-label. But surprisingly, and often amusingly, at first kids do not think of gender as a permanent state of being. They lack what psychologists call "gender constancy" (Ruble et al., 2006). A funny example: I asked my two and a half year old great niece, who madly loved the color pink at the time, what she wanted to be when she grew up. Loudly and proudly, she announced, "A pony!" "Why," I asked, "do you want to be a pony?" "Because I really like ponies," she logically explained. In the United States, children aged 3–5 years learn that one's sex remains stable over time. But they may not understand that being male or female (leaving aside for the moment the question of transgendered children) is a fixed property until they are as old as seven.

There are many details still to be worked out, but this is the general lesson, gleaned from studies done for the most part in the United States and Western Europe: the development of gender identity proceeds over several years. In the beginning, infants process visual, tactile, and auditory information. We presume that these varied sensory stimuli affect brain development, as intermodal connections form. With time and familiarity, infants and toddlers observe culturally frequent tropes and record them in their rapidly developing brains. Men don't wear lipstick. Women don't use hammers. With time, what begin as relatively simple sensory skills transform into more complex capabilities; as a sense of self, independent from parents, emerges, toddlers associate their newly emerging independent selves with the culturally specific gender knowledge they are acquiring at more or less the same time. (Remember that the "terrible twos" are all about self-assertion and the establishment of independent identity.) Even more sophisticated concepts such as body constancy are the last to appear.

Gender roles don't develop in a vacuum. For instance, family structure matters. Three year old boys with older brothers or girls with older
sisters have been found to be more boy boys or more girl girls (i.e. more
sex-typed) compared to only children of the same sex. There are two
ways to become more sex-typed—either do more of the same sex behaviors or less of the other sex behaviors. In other words, a little girl can
become girlier by playing even more with dolls, or by holding the doll-
play steady but playing less often with trucks. It turns out that having an
older brother linked to both more masculine *and* less feminine behavior
in both boys and girls. But boys with older sisters kept the same level of
male-typed play while also playing more often in female-typical ways.
Girls with older sisters did not play more with dolls, but they did play
less often with trucks (Rust, Golombok, Hines, Johnston, & Golding,
2000). (See Table 5.3.)

Parental characteristics also correlate with sex-typed behaviors. One
study found, for example, that more educated mothers or parents who
adhered less strictly to traditional sex roles had children who were
themselves less sex-typed. Maternal tobacco or alcohol use correlated
with more masculine-typical behaviors while more timid mothers
linked to less male-typical behavior (Hines, Johnston, Golombok, Rust,
Stevens, & Golding, 2002). Studies such as these, which correlate
aspects of the family with gender role development, suggest that quite a

Table 5.3 Sibling effects

	Older brother	Older sister	No sibling
Girl	Less sex typed: more masculine and less feminine	More sex typed: less masculine but not more feminine	Intermediate: > than girls with other sex siblings but less than girls with same sex siblings
Boy	More sex typed: more masculine and less feminine	Less sex typed: more feminine but not less masculine	Intermediate: > than boys with other sex siblings but less than boys with same sex siblings

number of environmental and cultural variations contribute to small individual differences in gender development. They probably also contribute to the population level differences in gender roles and interests. To date, however, what we have are correlations, not causal chains. In the future it will probably be possible to demonstrate some causal relationships. But the hard truth is that there are probably so many contributing streams, and they probably interact in so many different ways, that we will never have a single story to tell about gender development. Even within the same culture, the future of gender will consist of individual case studies that illuminate our questions. But I predict no specific universal story.

There is one important aspect of this tale about which we know virtually nothing. John Money emphasized that at birth the surrounding adults recognized the infant's genitalia and used that information to treat the child as either a boy or a girl. He also suggested that children themselves develop masculine or feminine body images depending on their external genitalia. Body image certainly develops and depends on self exploration and the recognition of sensations of self touch and touch by others—to begin with probably adult touch involved with cleaning and diapering—and eventually visual feedback from self examination and by comparison to other children's and to adult genitalia. The sensory feedback signals the brain and establishes actual neural connections. These connections between periphery (the body) and center (the brain) become a neural map of body parts, including the genitals. (It is this map which accounts for phenomena such as phantom limb sensations—pain and other sensations experienced by amputees as if belonging to the missing limb.) Which specific events contribute to the development of a child's body image and then later at puberty to an adult self image are virtually unknown. Nor, given the taboo against studying genital touch in children, is this something we are ever likely to study in a scientifically systematic way. Yet, given our wish to understand what happens when chromosomal, gonadal, hormonal, and genital sex disagree with body image and gender identity (childhood transgender identity), we would do well to understand more than we do at the moment.

What about Gender Variant Children?

By the age of 2–3 years children learn to correctly identify the sex of others (Martin et al., 2002; Martin, Ruble, & Szkrybalo, 2004) but even before then—as early as 18 months—they begin to develop an awareness of gender appropriate roles (Serbin et al., 2002). While some scientists believe that gender identity formation results from the effects of prenatal hormones on the brain, many cognitive and social psychologists understand gender identity formation to result from a process of learning, cognitive development, and social reinforcement (Bandura & Bussey, 2004; Martin et al., 2002). Individuals with clinically defined gender identity disorders have been the subject of much study, which, in turn, provides fodder for arguments concerning the role of biology in gender identity formation. A rich literature exists concerning adults with gender identity variance—sometimes called transsexual, sometimes transgender (Meyerowitz, 2002; Stryker & Whittle, 2006); the transgender movements (Feinberg, 1996, 1998) and various positive presentations of the self as gender outlaws (Bornstein, 1994) are complex. In keeping with this book's theme of understanding through the study of developmental process, I mostly focus on the emergence of gender identity variability in very young children.

The popular press and many adult transsexuals often define a transsexual as a genetically and developmentally normal (in the anatomical sense) person who believes him or herself to be trapped in the "wrong" body. Thus by definition the phenomenon involves a sense of self (identity) that is invisible and seems to have no origins in anatomical measures of intersexuality. The commonly sought treatment is to "correct" the anatomy to conform to the identity. Hormone treatments to bring the body's biochemistry into line accompany surgical transformations of the genitals and alterations in secondary sex characteristics. The latter include mastectomy in Female to Male (FtM) transformations, and surgery on the Adam's apple and body hair removal in Male to Female (MtF) transformations.

Because of the strength of their desire to bring anatomy and identity into synch, and because often they recall wanting since childhood to *be* the other sex, many adult transsexuals believe their condition to have a biological origin. Many suspect that there is something unusual about their own brain development. Indeed, a few post-mortem studies of brains of MtF transsexuals claim to prove that a region of the hypothalamus in the brain is "female-like" in Mtfs, a finding which they take as evidence of a biological cause for this unusual gender identity (Kruijver, Zhou, Pool, Hofman, Gooren, & Swaab, 2000; Zhou, Hofman, Gooren, & Swaab, 1995). Others, however, provide evidence that the cross hormone therapy undergone by the MtFs in these earlier studies produced the brain differences found (cited in Lawrence, 2007). At this time, then there is little substantial evidence to support the idea that adult MtFs have feminized brains which caused their desire to change their anatomy to fit their identity (Lawrence, 2007). (For further information on definitions of and research on adult transsexuals, see Lawrence, 2008.)

New brain studies, however, continue to appear and each one improves a bit on the methodology. Table 5.4 samples a few recent publications and identifies some of the difficulties such studies face. It also illustrates something fundamental—and at times problematic—about how we conduct scientific research. Pretty much all researchers have a model, or a theory, or a point of view, which they use to structure their research questions and methods. In the case of transgender brain studies, the underlying model is that gender identity is part of brain sex, and quite possibly shaped by prenatal hormone exposures. The counter hypothesis in the eyes of many would be that social interactions during infancy or childhood cause gender identity discomfort. These alternatives shape the thinking of the studies cited in Table 5.4. The logic seems clear to these scientists: if there are anatomical differences in the brains of MtF or FtM people that mirror differences found in non-transgendered men and women, *and* if the differences are not the result of unusual hormone changes caused by disease or by the treatments used on transitioning from one sex to the other, then they reason that the only possible explanation is that gender identity is inborn (Kruijver et al., 2000; Rametti, Carrillo, Gómez-Gil, Junque, Segovia, Gomez, et al., 2011a; Rametti, Carrillo, Gómez-Gil, Junque, Zubiarre-Elorza, Segovia, et al., 2011b).

Table 5.4 What we know about brain differences in adult transsexuals (selected examples)

Type	Study method and reference	Brain region	Finding	Possible interpretations	Author's conclusions
Male to Female	Post-mortem; (Kruijver, Zhou, Pool, Hofman, Gooren, & Swaab, 2000)	Bed nucleus of the stria terminalis (BSTc)	Men have 2X more somatostatin neurons than women; MtF individuals more like female number	• Results influenced by medical history which led to death • Results influenced by hormone treatments for sex change procedure • Results due to neuronal plasticity resulting from experience of living as women and girls • Neurobiological differences that parallel normal sex differences cause gender identity disorder	"The present findings of somatostatin neuronal sex differences in the BSTc and its sex reversal in the transsexual brain clearly support the paradigm that in transsexuals sexual differentiation of the brain and genitals may go into opposite directions and point to a neurobiological basis of gender identity disorder" (p. 2034)

| Male to Female | DTI imaging on living subjects who had *not* received hormone treatments (Rametti, Carrillo, Gómez-Gil, Junque, Zubiarre-Elorza, Segovia, et al., 2011b) | Microstructure of white matter in specific regions of the brain | There are sex differences in adults for the observed regions; MtF fall halfway between male and female patterns | • Results due to neuronal plasticity resulting from experience of living as women and girls

• Neurobiological differences that parallel normal sex differences cause gender identity disorder

• Cannot rule out prior black market self hormone treatment | Some of the white matter tracts don't finish masculinization before the individual seeks treatment |

(Continued Overleaf)

Table 5.4 Continued

Type	Study method and reference	Brain region	Finding	Possible interpretations	Author's conclusions
Female to Male	DTI imaging on living subjects who had *not* received hormone treatments (Rametti, Carrillo, Gómez-Gil, Junque, Segovia, Gomez, et al., 2011a)	Microstructure of white matter in specific regions of the brain	There are sex differences in adults for the observed regions; FtM resemble the male patterns	• Results due to neuronal plasticity resulting from experience of living as men and boys • Neurobiological differences that parallel normal sex differences cause gender identity disorder • Cannot rule out prior black market self hormone treatment	"There are a priori structural brain differences suggesting masculinization of untreated FtM transsexuals" (p. 203)

But what about more dynamic models (Fausto-Sterling et al., 2011a, 2011b)? For several decades neuroscientists have documented the whys and wherefores of neural plasticity. Existing neurons change their connections; new neurons are born, and all this happens as a result of how the body interacts day to day in the physical world. If a dynamic nervous system that is shaped by the environment is the starting framework, then essential questions about transgender embodiment have yet to be asked, crucial studies have yet to be conducted. Consider the differences in white matter tracks found in FtM transsexuals. One region, called the superior longitudinal fasciculus (SLF) is part of a brain network important for spatial awareness. As the authors of this report on FtMs note, these white matter tracts develop continuously until the late twenties. Another region of difference, the corticospinal tract, requires motor experience to develop properly (Rametti et al., 2011a). But because neuroplasticity is not an essential part of their model, these facts do not take on the level of meaning that would lead to studies designed to examine the development or emergence of anatomical differences in the brains of men or women. In short, the science you do depends on the model of the body you start with.

If studies of adult transsexuals have yet to offer convincing evidence of a biological origin of the phenomenon, then maybe reports of gender variant children, some barely more than 2 years old, do. The general argument is that only biology could explain such an early origin of gender variance. The American Psychiatric Association first listed a mental illness called Gender Identity Disorder of Childhood (GIDC) in its Diagnostic and Statistical Manual (DSM) in 1980 (Martin, 2008). Since then the diagnostic criteria have undergone a variety of modifications. DSM-IV states that GIDC children display a constellation of behaviors:

(1) a strong and persistent cross-gender identification ... (2) persistent discomfort with his or her sex ... (3) disturbance not concurrent with a physical intersex condition and (4) disturbance causes clinically significant distress or impairment in social, occupational or other important areas of functioning.
(cited in Zucker & Cohen-Kettenis, 2008: 384)

The actual prevalence of children with the above constellation of behaviors is difficult to assess, especially because of the range of variability in gender non-conforming behaviors in children who, in the end, do not have identity issues. Nevertheless, some estimate that between 0.9 and 1.7 percent of boys and girls in a general North American population wish to be a member of the opposite sex (Zucker & Cohen-Kettenis, 2008).

In the health care system gender non-conformance rises to the level of mental illness when children are referred to mental health clinics for treatment. Parents seek clinical help for several reasons. Sometimes the child is anxious and distressed, occasionally to the extent that he or she tries to harm him or herself. And the parents are also in distress about their child's gender variance, sometimes because they fear their child will grow up to become homosexual, and usually about other life stresses. But not all kids are distressed to the same degree. And some parents value and admire their gender variant children. More than anything these latter adults seek support and advice as they help their kids navigate some very difficult terrain (Hill, Menvielle, Sica, & Johnson, 2010; Menvielle & Hill, 2011). About five times as many boys as girls are referred to one well-known Canadian clinic while the ratio is about 3:1 boys:girls in a prominent Dutch clinic. At these clinics, gender non-conforming children are referred between the ages of 3 and 6 years (Zucker & Cohen-Kettenis, 2008).

More boys than girls

Note that we often slip, especially in casual conversations, between the idea of gender non-conformity (girls who like boys' toys, boys who like girls' toys) and gender identity disorder, as defined by psychiatrists and clinical psychologists. Worse yet, shrinks and counselors disagree about whether there is any mental disorder at all, or whether boys who want to be girls (and vice versa) are merely one end on a spectrum of totally normal gender variability.

In one recent case, publicized on US television, the child in question began exhibiting gender non-conforming behavior by his or her second year of age (Goldberg, 2007; Winfrey, 2004). Experts and lay people alike disagree about the proper course to follow with such children—intervene to make them more comfortable with their natal sex, work with family and school systems to accommodate the gender non-conformity, and/or provide online and in person support groups (Langer & Martin, 2004; Martin, 2008; Menvielle & Hill, 2011; Menvielle & Tuerk, 2002; Menvielle, Tuerk, & Perrin, 2005; Spiegel, 2008a, 2008b; Zucker & Cohen-Kettenis, 2008). But regardless of which path is followed, is there something to be learned about the biology of gender from gender identity variance in very young children?

The fact that childhood gender identity variability can appear as early as the third year of life is not itself evidence that the cause is biological, and certainly not that it comes from a malfunction of fetal hormonal sex. Indeed, given what we have just discussed about the dynamics of gender knowledge acquisition we know that the assimilation of gender skills starts before the appearance of gender identity variation, and thus, at least logically, the learning and assimilation process itself could be one of the seats on which GID sits. We should also remember that the labeled outcome—gender identity disorder—could have different origins in different children. Although right now we approach GID as if it were a single entity, the single endpoint will probably turn out to have a number of different paths leading up to it.

Indeed a recent assessment of 53 adolescents—both natal boys and natal girls who sought treatment at the Gender Identity Clinic in Amsterdam, the Netherlands, between the ages of 7 and 10, turned up two equally frequent sub-groups which they called "persisters" and "desisters." The labels are pretty much self explanatory. Persisters continued throughout adolescence to have gender dysphoria. The physiological maturation of their bodies caused them great distress, and although they had managed pretty well in childhood to be accepted by their peers, during adolescence they became more and more isolated. In contrast, the desisters gradually became more comfortable with their natal bodies and more interested in gender conforming activities. If their peers did not know about their earlier non-conforming history, they assimilated surprisingly well into their new social milieu as gender conforming teens (Steensma, Biemond, Boer, & Cohen-Kettenis, 2011).

The Dutch Gender Identity Clinic researchers interviewed persisters and desisters at some length and found that although their childhood cross-gender behaviors were indistinguishable, differences existed between the two groups. In the beginning, i.e. around the age of 5, neither persisters nor desisters gave their gender identity much thought. But by age 6 or 7 both groups started to identify with their non-natal sex and feel uncomfortable with their birth sex. Here is where the difference appears. Persisters actually believed themselves to *be* the other sex. The desisters thought of themselves as girlish boys or boyish girls who only *wished* they were the other sex. This difference carried over as the children grew older to their feelings about their bodies. Persisters indicated great discomfort because their bodies did not match their feelings of which sex they felt they were. Desisters, on the other hand, accepted the bodies they were born into.

Thus it seems likely that there are at least two—and I will predict the uncovering of several more—paths leading to gender variant feelings and behaviors in children. What might some of the elements guiding the development of these paths be? Newborn genital sex (male or female) precedes the appearance and subsequent elaboration of either masculine or feminine gender expression. Humans code such expressions culturally, that is what counts as masculine or feminine differs in different cultures. Furthermore, the differences are graded rather than absolute. Whereas usually the genitals are clearly dimorphic, masculinity and femininity form intermixing, non-exclusive gradients. A toddler may primarily like trucks and male playmates, but may have a favorite girlfriend and be totally attached to a stuffed bear that *he* cannot sleep without. Or, *she* may really love to play with her doll house, but also race around shooting imaginary laser guns. Cultural standards of femininity and masculinity change over time. In my youth (which was several light years ago) it would have been very *un*-feminine for a girl to be a sports fanatic and compete aggressively and physically in sports such as basketball or soccer. Today female athletes can be successful, glamorous, *and* loud and aggressive during competition.

At any rate, genitalia precede masculine or feminine gender expression, which in turn precedes gender identity formation. The latter begins to appear in the third year and solidifies and clarifies over several subsequent years. Most commonly male genitalia, masculine gender expression, and male gender identity seem to follow the one from the other. The same too for female genitalia, gender expression, and gender identity. Less frequently, a boy (identified by his genitalia) develops a gender expression that is graded more toward the feminine end of the expression spectrum, or a girl more toward the masculine end. Most of the time, such children still develop an internal gender identity that matches their genitalia. But for GID kids genitalia and chromosomes seem, as it were, to be the "odd man out." Gender expression and gender identity match one another but are at variance with the child's chromosomes and genitalia.

Why? To be clear, we really don't know. I speculate that individual variations in neurosensory development might combine with particular family psychodynamics, and that such a combination somehow disrupts the usual developmental patterns for gender identity formation (Fausto-Sterling, 2012). Martin (2008) reviews several competing psychodynamic explanations of early childhood gender variance but neither these, nor the competing idea that families of gender variant kids are reasonably healthy, have been supported with data "hard" enough to convince research psychologists that one of them is correct (Menvielle et al., 2005).

More to the point, however, is that to structure the debate in terms of biology *versus* psychology misses some essential features of child development. In recent years dynamic systems theorists have offered compelling accounts of human development that emphasize how behavior becomes embodied (Fausto-Sterling, 2000; Hayles, 1993; Thelen, 1995, 2000; Thelen & Smith, 1994). In the case of gender variant children, it is significant that the variation becomes visible through a developmental window that also features the establishment of gender identity and a sense of gender permanence (Fagot & Leinbach, 1989, 1993; Fagot, Leinbach, & Hagan, 1986; Fagot, Leinbach, & O'Boyle, 1992; Martin et al., 2002; Ruble & Martin, 1998).

Alterations in developmental timing of gender role knowledge and identity formation, chance fixations that happen to be gender specific (one child I knew went through a phase at aged 1.5 to 2 when he carried a paint brush with him at all times—he outgrew this obsession) and get fixed or fixated upon rather than outgrown—any of these general developmental possibilities, in a sense accidents of chance or timing, could start small but with repetition, quite literally become embodied, that is become a persistent feature of an individual's identity and personality. At the level of neurophysiology, we presume that these features function via neural networks within the brain. Individual variation in neural development could influence initial fixations that become associated with developing knowledge of a gendered world. Developing more dynamic hypotheses and new experimental paradigms, ones in which neural development (and thus behaviors, identities, and preferences) *result from* initial behavioral exploration should be on the agenda of the next generation of researchers.

Much of the controversy over early treatment of GIDC children concerns the possibility that gender variant children will become homosexual adults (Bem, 2008; Corbett, 1993, 1996; Green, 2008; Martin, 2008; Zucker, 2008). The idea that early emerging gender non-conforming behaviors must be "biological" is used to support the notion that adult homosexuality has a biological cause. There is one important bit of slippage in this argument; GIDC is an example of extreme gender variance. Gender non-conforming behaviors, however, are quite common, and while many adult homosexuals retrospectively associate them with a later emergence of homosexual desire, they are a less striking form of behavior than GIDC. Nevertheless it does appear that many of the gender variant kids who adopt the gender identity of their natal sex become homosexual or bisexual. In Steensma's study, the children who persisted in their gender variance also had same natal sex attractions in adolescence. But since they thought of themselves as "the other" sex, they defined these attractions as heterosexual ones. Clearly, there is more to be understood about the relationship between gender roles, gender identity, and sexual preference (Steensma et al., 2011).

The relationships between gender, anatomical sex, and sexuality are complex. Theo Sandfort attributes the origin in American psychology of the idea that homosexual men are feminine and lesbians masculine to the 1936 work of Lewis M. Terman and Catherine C. Miles (Sandfort, 2005). Although Terman and Miles identified homosexual men who did not fit these patterns of opposites, they failed to theorize about masculine gay men. Subsequent citations of their work also ignored this theoretical complication, giving birth to the unquestioned link between male homosexuality and femininity. Practicing psychoanalyst Ken Corbett writes that "Calling gay men feminine neither sufficiently problematizes their experience of gender nor adequately captures the vicissitudes of gender." He argues that "male homosexuality is a differently structured masculinity, not a simulated femininity" (Corbett, 1993: 345). Despite these complexities, arguments about the biological basis of homosexuality lean heavily on the relationship between GIDC and later homosexuality, and in recent years biological theories have come to rest as well on somewhat more direct evidence, which we address in the next chapter.

Further Reading

Consortium on the Management of Disorders of Sex Development. (2006). *Clinical Guidelines for the Management of Disorders of Sex Development in Childhood.* Copyright © 2006 Intersex Society of North America. http://www.dsdguidelines.org/htdocs/clinical/index.html

Consortium on the Management of Disorders of Sex Development. (2006). *Handbook for Parents.* Retrieved from: http://www.dsdguidelines.org/htdocs/parents/index.html, accessed December 8, 2011.

Dreger, A. (2009). Gender Identity Disorder in childhood: Inconclusive advice to parents. *Hastings Center Report*, 39(1), 26–29.

Dreger, A. (2010). "Pink Boys with Puppy Dog Tails." Monday, December 6, http://sexresearchhoneypot.blogspot.com/2010/12/pink-boys-with-puppy-dog-tails.html

Ehrensaft, D. (2011). "I'm a Prius": a child case of a gender/ethnic hybrid. *Journal of Gay and Lesbian Mental Health*, 15, 46–57.

Fausto-Sterling, A. (2012). The dynamic development of gender variability. *Journal of Homosexuality*, in press.

Karkazis, K. (2008) *Fixing Sex: Intersex, Medical Authority, and Lived Experience.* Durham, NC: Duke University Press.

Kessler, S. J., & McKenna, W. (1978). *Gender: An Ethnomethodological Approach.* New York: John Wiley & Sons.

Reis, E. (2009). *Bodies in Doubt: An American History of Intersex.* Baltimore, MD: Johns Hopkins University Press.

Stiles, Joan (2008). *The Fundamentals of Brain Development: Integrating Nature and Nurture.* Cambridge, MA: Harvard University Press.

Stryker, S., & Whittle, S. (2006). *The Transgender Studies Reader.* New York: Routledge.

Valentine, D. (2007). *Imagining Transgender: An Ethnography of a Category.* Durham, NC: Duke University Press.

Zucker, K. J., & Bradley, S. J. (1995). *Gender Identity Disorder and Psychosexual Problems in Children and Adolescents.* New York: Guilford Press.

6

THINKING ABOUT
HOMOSEXUALITY[1]

Sexuality Has a History

"The Gay" (as TV newscaster Rachel Maddow ironically calls it) is newsworthy. Gay marriage. Don't ask don't tell. The Gay Agenda. We can't escape it. It seems as if we know so much about the topic. But do we? Is it one thing? Many things? Is it the same in men as in women? What does it have to do with sex and gender? How does it develop? Who knows more about human desire—biologists or poets?

Not all cultures—either contemporary or historically—structure gender and sexuality the way we do (see Figure 6.1). Many historians mark the seventeenth and eighteenth centuries as periods of great change in our concepts of sex and sexuality. During this time a notion of legal equality replaced the feudal exercise of arbitrary power given by divine right. As the historian Michel Foucault saw it, society still required some form of discipline. A growing capitalism needed new methods to control the "insertion of bodies into the machinery of production and the adjustment of the phenomena of population to economic processes" (Foucault, 1978: 141 cited in Fausto-Sterling, 2000).

Foucault argued that "a biopolitics of the population" emerged during the early nineteenth century as pioneer social scientists began to develop the survey and statistical methods needed to supervise and manage births and mortality, life expectancy and longevity. Foucault gave

Source: Diane DiMassa for the author.

Figure 6.1 Constructing sex and gender: a political, religious, and scientific history.

"discipline" a double meaning. On the one hand, it implied a form of control or punishment; on the other, it referred to an academic body of knowledge—the discipline of history or biology. The disciplinary knowledge developed in the fields of embryology, endocrinology, surgery, psychology, and biochemistry has encouraged physicians to

attempt to control the very gender of the body by making categories—
little cubbies we can put people in based on, for example, their patterns
of sexual expression. If the groupings are stable and easily measured,
then the various medical and psychological disciplines can study them.
Consider, for instance, a television news magazine segment about
married women who "discovered," often in their forties, that they were
lesbian. The show framed the discussion around the idea that a woman
who has sex with men must be heterosexual, while a woman who falls in
love with another woman must be lesbian. On this show there seemed
to be only these two cubbyholes. Even though the women interviewed
had had active and satisfying sex lives with their husbands and produced
and raised families, they knew that they must "be" lesbian the minute
they found themselves attracted to a woman. Furthermore, they felt it
likely that they must always have been lesbian without knowing it
(Strock, 1998).

The show portrayed sexual identity as a fundamental reality: a woman
is either inherently heterosexual or inherently lesbian. And the act of
coming out as a lesbian negated an entire lifetime of heterosexual
activity! Put this way, the depiction of sexuality sounds absurdly over-
simplified. Yet, it reflects deeply held beliefs—so deeply held, in fact,
that a great deal of scientific research (on animals as well as humans) is,
as we shall see momentarily, designed around this dichotomous
formulation.

The social organization and expression of human sexuality are neither
timeless nor universal. Historians struggle with how to understand what
people of an earlier era really felt or understood without pushing them
into categories of contemporary making but irrelevant for a life lived a
century ago. For example, the historian of science Barbara Duden
describes coming upon an eight-volume medical text. Written in the
eighteenth century by a practicing physician, the books describe over
1,800 cases involving diseases of women. Duden found herself unable to
use twentieth-century medical terms to reconstruct what illnesses these
women had. Instead she noticed "bits and pieces of medical theories that
would have been circulating, combined with elements from popular
culture; self-evident bodily perceptions appear alongside things that

struck [her] as utterly improbable" (1991: v). Duden describes her intellectual anguish as she became more and more determined to understand these eighteenth-century German female bodies on their own terms:

> To gain access to the inner, invisible bodily existence of these ailing women, I had to venture across the boundary that separates . . . the inner body beneath the skin, from the world around it . . . the body and its environment have been consigned to opposing realms: on the one side are the body, nature, and biology, stable and unchanging phenomena; on the other side are the social environment and history, realms of constant change. With the drawing of this boundary the body was expelled from history.
>
> (Duden, 1991: v, vi)

Many historians believe that our modern concepts of sex and desire first made their appearance in the nineteenth century. Some point to the year 1869, when a German legal reformer seeking to change antisodomy laws first publicly used the word "homosexuality" (Katz, 1995). Coining a new term did not magically create twentieth-century categories of sexuality, but the moment seems to mark the beginning of their gradual emergence. It was during those years that physicians began to publish case reports of homosexuality—the first in 1869 in a German publication specializing in psychiatric and nervous illness (Hansen, 1989, 1992). As the scientific literature grew, specialists emerged to collect and systematize the narratives. The now-classic works of Krafft-Ebing and Havelock Ellis completed the transfer of homosexual behaviors from publicly accessible activities to ones managed at least in part by medicine (Ellis, 1913; Krafft-Ebing, 1892).

The emerging definitions of homo- and heterosexuality were built on a two-sex model of masculinity and femininity. The Victorians, for example, contrasted the sexually aggressive male with the sexually indifferent female. But this created a mystery. If only men felt active desire, how could two women develop a mutual sexual interest? The answer: one of the women had to be an invert, someone with markedly masculine attributes. This same logic applied to male homosexuals, who were seen as more effeminate than heterosexual men. These concepts linger in late-twentieth-century studies of homosexual behaviors in rodents. A lesbian rat is she who mounts; a gay male rat is he who responds to being mounted.

This forming identity contributed to its own medical rendering. Men (and later women) who identified themselves as homosexual sought medical help and understanding. And as medical reports proliferated, homosexuals used them to paint their own self-descriptions. "By helping to give large numbers of people an identity and a name, medicine also helped to shape these people's experience and change their behavior, creating not just a new disease, but a new species of person, 'the modern homosexual'" (Hansen, 1992: 125). In 1892, heterosexuality crossed the ocean to America, where a consensus developed among medical men that "heterosexual referred to a normal 'other-sex' Eros. [The doctors] proclaimed a new heterosexual separatism—an erotic apartheid that forcefully segregated the sex normals from the sex perverts" (Katz, 1995: 16). Through the 1930s the concept of heterosexuality fought its way into the public consciousness, and, by World War II, heterosexuality seemed a permanent feature of the sexual landscape.

The above historians emphasize discontinuity between historical periods. They believe that looking "for general laws about sexuality and its historical evolution will be defeated by the sheer variety of past thought and behavior" (Nye, 1998: 4). But some disagree. The historian John Boswell, for instance, applied Kinsey's classification scheme to ancient Greece. For him, the existence of categories such as the malle (feminine man) or the tribade (masculine woman) shows that homosexual bodies or essences have existed across the centuries. Boswell acknowledged that humans organized and interpreted sexual behaviors differently in different historical eras. But he suggested that a similar range of bodies predisposed to particular sexual activities existed then and now. "Constructions and context shape the articulation of sexuality," he insists, "but they do not efface recognition of erotic preference as a potential category" (Boswell, 1990: 22, 26). Boswell implied that we are quite possibly born with particular sexual inclinations wired into our bodies. The acquisition of culture shows us how to express our inborn desires, he argued, but did not create them.

The debate about history continues. What we conclude about people's past experiences depends to a large extent on how much we believe that our analytical categories transcend time and place. Suppose for a minute that we had a few time-traveling clones—genetically identical humans living in ancient Greece, in seventeenth-century Europe, and in the contemporary United States. Boswell would say that if a particular clone was homosexual in ancient Greece, he would also be homosexual in the seventeenth century or today (Figure 6.2, Model A). The fact that gender structures differ in different times and places might shape the invert's defiance, but would not create it. Halperin, however, would argue that there is no guarantee that the modern clone of an ancient Greek heterosexual would also be heterosexual. Despite surface similarities, we cannot know whether yesterday's tribade is today's butch or whether the middle-aged Greek male lover is today's pedophile (Figure 6.2, Model B).

[handwritten margin note: Do we know which is true?]

If not History, What about Anthropology?

While historians have looked to the past to find out if human sexuality is inborn or socially determined, anthropologists have pursued the same questions in their studies of sexual behaviors, roles, and expressions in contemporary cultures. There seem to be two general patterns. Some cultures, like our own, define a permanent role for those who engage in same sex coupling—"institutionalized homosexuality," in Mary McIntosh's terminology (McIntosh, 1968).

In contrast are societies in which all adolescent boys, as part of an expected growth process, engage in genital acts with older men. These associations may be brief and highly ritualized or last for several years. Here oral-genital contact between two males does not signify a permanent condition. Rather age and status define sexual expression (Vance, 1991). Anthropologists study vastly differing peoples and cultures with two goals in mind. First, they want to understand human variation—the diverse ways in which human beings organize society in order to eat and reproduce. Second, many anthropologists look for human universals.

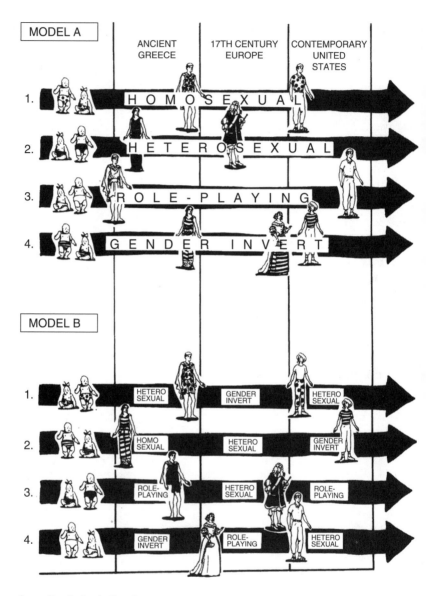

Source: Alyce Santoro for the author.

Figure 6.2 Model A: Reading essentialism from the historical record. A person with inborn homosexual tendencies would be homosexual, no matter what historical era. Model B: Reading
constructionism from the historical record. A person of a particular genetic make-up
might or might not become homosexual, depending on the cultural and historical period
in which he or she was raised.

Like historians, anthropologists are divided about how much information drawn from any one culture can tell us about another, or whether
underlying differences in the expression of sexuality matter more or less
than apparent commonalities. Despite such disagreements, anthropo-
logical data are, nevertheless, often deployed in arguments about the
nature of human sexuality (Davis & Whitten, 1987; Weinrich, 1987;
Weston, 1993).

Some find cross-cultural similarities. For instance, the anthropologist
Gil Herdt catalogs four primary cultural approaches to the organization
of human sexuality. *Age-structured homosexuality*, such as that found in
ancient Greece, also appears in some modern cultures in which adolescent boys go through a developmental period in which they are isolated
with older males and perform fellatio on a regular basis. Such acts are
understood to be part of the normal process of becoming an adult
heterosexual. In *gender-reversed homosexuality*, "same-sex activity
involves a reversal of normative sex-role comportment: males dress and
act as females, and females dress and behave as males" (Herdt, 1990:
222). Herdt finds *role-specialized homosexuality* in cultures that sanction
same-sex activity only for people who play a particular social role, such
as a shaman. Role-specialized homosexuality contrasts sharply with our
own cultural creation: *the modern gay movement.* To declare oneself "gay"
in the United States is to adopt an identity and to join a social and
sometimes political movement.

Anthropologists also face theoretical difficulties when they turn their
attention to the relationships between gender and systems of social
power. During the 1970s European and North American feminist
activists hoped that anthropologists could provide empirical data to
support their political arguments for gender equality. If, somewhere in
the world, egalitarian societies existed, wouldn't that imply that our own
social structures were not inevitable? Alternatively, what if women in
every culture known to humankind had a subordinate status? Didn't
such cross-cultural similarity mean, as more than one writer suggested,
that women's secondary standing must be biologically ordained?

When feminist anthropologists searched for cultures sporting the
banner of equity, they did not return with happy tidings. Most thought,

as the feminist anthropologist Sherry Ortner writes, "that men were in some way or other 'the first sex'" (Ortner, 1996: 146). But critiques of these early cross-cultural analyses mounted, and in the 1990s some prominent feminist anthropologists reassessed the issue. Ortner thinks that argument about the universality of sexual inequality has continued for more than two decades because anthropologists assumed that each society would be internally consistent, an expectation she now believes to be unreasonable: "no society or culture is totally consistent. Every society/culture has some axes of male prestige and some of female, some of gender equality, and some (sometimes many) axes of prestige that have nothing to do with gender." The problem in the past has been that all of us were trying to pigeonhole each case. Now she argues instead that "the most interesting thing about any given case is precisely the multiplicity of logics operating, of discourses being spoken, of practices of prestige and power in play" (ibid.: 146). If one attends to the dynamics, the contradictions, and minor themes, Ortner believes, one can see both the currently dominant system and the potential for minor themes to become major ones.

Feminists also have incorrigible propositions, and a central one has been that all cultures, as the Nigerian anthropologist Oyeronke Oyewumi writes, "organize their social world through a perception of human bodies as male or female" (Oyewumi, 1998: 1053). In taking European and North American feminists to task over this proposition, Oyewumi shows how the imposition of a system of gender—in this case, through colonialism followed by scholarly imperialism—can alter our understandings of ethnic and racial difference. In her own detailed analysis of Yoruba culture, Oyewumi finds that relative age is a far more significant social organizer. Yoruba pronouns, for example, do not indicate sex, but rather who is older or younger than the speaker.

If Yoruba intellectuals had constructed the original scholarship on Yorubaland, Oyewumi thinks that "seniority would have been privileged over gender" (ibid.: 1061). Seeing Yoruba society through the lens of seniority rather than gender would have two important effects. First, if Euro-American scholars learned about Nigeria from Yoruba anthropologists, our own belief systems about the universality of gender might change. Second, the articulation of a seniority-based vision of social organization among the Yoruba would, presumably, reinforce such social structures.

Thus historians and anthropologists disagree about how to interpret human sexuality across cultures and history. Philosophers even dispute the validity of the words "homosexual" and "heterosexual"—the very terms of the argument (Stein, 1998). But wherever they fall along the social constructionist spectrum, most argue from the assumption that there is a fundamental split between nature and culture, between "real bodies" and their cultural interpretations. This split, however, may not be a good way to look at the problem. Bodily experiences are brought into being by our development in particular cultures and historical periods. As we grow and develop, we literally, not just "discursively" (that is, through language and cultural practices), construct our bodies, incorporating experience into our very flesh. If this is correct, the distinctions between the physical and the social body start to erode, something we illustrate with examples throughout this book.

O.K., O.K. but What about Biology?

At a recent scientific meeting on the biology of sex differences a top scientist in the field averred to an audience of several hundred rapt listeners that, with regard to sex and sexual desire, men are really very simple. They are either heterosexual and thus masculine in interests and desires or homosexual and thus feminized in interests and desires. Hardly any men, he said, are intermediate in desire. Women, the speaker agreed, were probably not so simple and so he focused more on what we think we know about men.

But what, exactly *are* masculine and feminine men? One need only look at images of seventeenth-century men, dressed in frills and wigs, with rouge reddening their cheeks, to know that our ideas about masculinity and femininity have changed over the years. More recently (from roughly 1967 to the present) scientists who study sexuality have also gradually changed their conceptualization of masculine and feminine sexuality.

1660–1670

These clothes were high fashion in Europe in the late 1650s but did not become so in England until Charles II's Restoration in 1660.

Such dress was over-decorated and rather absurd: brief doublets with short sleeves revealed billowing shirts; 'petticoat' breeches terminated in frilled knee canons. Ribbons proliferated: on cuffs, at the waistline and, called 'fancies', on the petticoat. Lace trimmed every edge from cloak to bib. Periwig and peruke began their long reign. *Facing page.* In about 1665 in England, the vest or waistcoat, with tunic or coat, superceded the former style.

Black hats were heavily laden with coloured ostrich feathers.

The bib, *always* falling from the high collar of the doublet was almost universal. Some bibs were of plain lawn or linen and others were made entirely of heavy lace, or linen with borders of varying depth. This border was either pleated at the side or made in a curved shape. With very deep bibs the bobble-tasselled band-strings were often hidden.

Figure 6.3 Seventeenth-century masculine attire.

In the late 1960s scientists viewed sexual intercourse (penile-vaginal penetration) as the unique spot where masculine and feminine met (as seen in Figure 6.4, reprinted from Jordan-Young, 2010). In theory, masculine men desired only women and their only goal for sex was the sex act itself. Feminine women were understood to desire only men, but their goals for the sex act were love and motherhood. Beyond that, a person with masculine sexuality masturbated, actively pursued sexual contact, had a high libido, had erotic dreams, had multiple sex partners, and was aroused by visual imagery. Theoretically, a person with feminine sexuality did not masturbate, focused on their loved one, was monogamous, romantic, had no erotic dreams, and was aroused only by direct touch. This understanding of masculine and feminine sexuality shaped research on both hetero and homosexuality during the 1960s and 1970s in very specific ways—of which more in a moment.

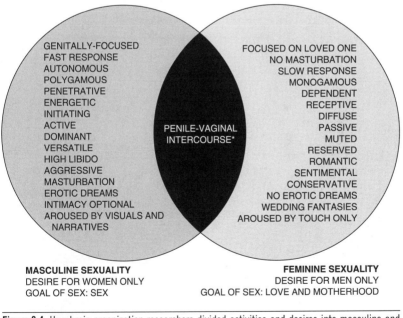

MASCULINE SEXUALITY
DESIRE FOR WOMEN ONLY
GOAL OF SEX: SEX

FEMININE SEXUALITY
DESIRE FOR MEN ONLY
GOAL OF SEX: LOVE AND MOTHERHOOD

GENITALLY-FOCUSED
FAST RESPONSE
AUTONOMOUS
POLYGAMOUS
PENETRATIVE
ENERGETIC
INITIATING
ACTIVE
DOMINANT
VERSATILE
HIGH LIBIDO
AGGRESSIVE
MASTURBATION
EROTIC DREAMS
INTIMACY OPTIONAL
AROUSED BY VISUALS AND NARRATIVES

PENILE-VAGINAL INTERCOURSE*

FOCUSED ON LOVED ONE
NO MASTURBATION
SLOW RESPONSE
MONOGAMOUS
DEPENDENT
RECEPTIVE
DIFFUSE
PASSIVE
MUTED
RESERVED
ROMANTIC
SENTIMENTAL
CONSERVATIVE
NO EROTIC DREAMS
WEDDING FANTASIES
AROUSED BY TOUCH ONLY

Figure 6.4 How brain organization researchers divided activities and desires into masculine and feminine in their early studies, roughly 1967 through 1980.

*Penile-vaginal intercourse should be understood as a "meeting-point" for masculine and feminine sexuality in this model, not an overlapping element.

Around 1980 things changed. It is possible that the sexual revolution brought about by widespread availability of birth control, increases in the divorce rate, and other large social changes account for the changes in the structure of sexual science. But regardless of cause, scientists began to see feminine sexuality as more active and diverse than they had in earlier decades. Whereas previously masculinity and femininity only overlapped in the desire for sexual intercourse, since the early 1980s they have evolved many similarities (Figure 6.5, reprinted from Jordan-Young, 2010). For researchers, human (rather than male or female) sexuality began to take center stage. While acknowledging differences of degree, researchers began to consider that both men and women have multiple partners, erotic dreams, frequent sexual activity, and masturbate (Jordan-Young, 2010).

How do current ideas about masculine and feminine desire map onto our thinking about homosexuality? Social anthropologist Rebecca Jordan-Young focuses on several interconnected issues (Table 6.1). Studies differ in their definitional choices, and the choice of definition has consequences. It is the old apples and oranges problem. Not all studies on homosexuality and its origins can be compared, making it

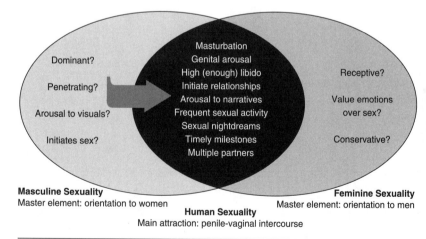

Figure 6.5 Masculine and feminine sexuality in later studies, from about 1980.

Table 6.1 Research issues in the study of homosexuality

What IS sexual orientation?

- Sex of actual partner
- Self description
- Sex of people one falls in love with
- Degree of desire (preference) for same or other sex partners

Is orientation toward:

- men versus women?
- one's own sex or the other sex?

Quantifying desire

- What are the cutpoints, i.e. how much interest in same sex sex disqualifies one from being scored as homosexual and vice versa?

hard to accumulate consistent evidence on the possible origins of human sexual orientation. In fact it even makes it difficult to agree on what might seem to be an elementary question: how frequent, in the human population, are the different forms of sexual orientation?

What *is* Sexual Orientation?

In the 1940s sex research pioneer Alfred Kinsey published a book reporting on his survey of sexual practices in a large sample of American men. He followed up, in 1953, with a similar volume on American women (Kinsey, Pomeroy, & Martin, 1948; Kinsey, Pomeroy, Martin, & Gebhard, 1953). These two volumes shocked many because they revealed widespread experimentation and variability in sexual practices. For better or for worse, Kinsey captured individual behaviors and thoughts and found that they often did not fit a neat picture of gay, straight, or bisexual. Kinsey wanted to assess the hetero-homosexual balance within each individual and so asked them about their activities and thoughts. (See Table 6.2 for Kinsey's Scale.) He did not intend to measure a person's underlying identity, but this has not prevented contemporary researchers from using the Kinsey Scale to label individuals as gay or straight; scholars, however, disagree about the utility and accuracy of defining homosexuality on the basis of the Kinsey Scale.

Table 6.2 The Kinsey Scale

0	Exclusively heterosexual
1	Predominantly heterosexual, only incidentally homosexual
2	Predominantly heterosexual, but more than incidentally homosexual
3	Equally heterosexual and homosexual
4	Predominantly homosexual, but more than incidentally heterosexual
5	Predominantly homosexual, only incidentally heterosexual
6	Exclusively homosexual
X	Asexual, non-sexual

The scale tells us how a researcher has rated an individual, but not which questions they asked to arrive at the rating. Indeed, different researchers are interested in different aspects of sexual expression. Some focus on actual behavior, some on personal identification as gay, straight, or bi, some on sexual fantasies, and others use composite assessments that include all of the above (Jordan-Young, 2010). All of which is to say that studies that use the Kinsey Scale don't all measure the same features of human behavior and desire. Apples and oranges . . .

When it first appeared, Kinsey's work shocked Americans; eventually the negative feedback led to a loss of funding for such studies. Thus there are long gaps during which little large scale research on sexuality occurred. But in the 1990s sociologist E. O. Laumann at the University of Chicago published two important volumes that detailed large, modern surveys of people's desires, behaviors, and identities. Some of his results can be found in Figures 6.6a and 6.6b. What is really interesting about Laumann's results is that only a small percentage of the men and women they surveyed were "consistent" in their sexuality—that is only a small number self-identified as gay, had same sex sexual encounters, *and* reported same sex desires. Some had same sex desire and behaviors but did not self-identify as gay. Others had same sex sexual encounters but reported neither same sex attraction or identity. A close study of the results represented in Figures 6.6a and 6.6b show that "homosexuality is a multidimensional phenomenon that has manifold

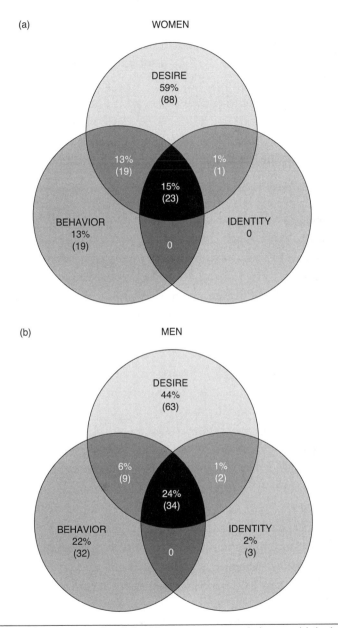

(a) WOMEN

Figure 6.6 (a) Among women, the relationships among same-sex desire, sexual behaviour with same-sex partners, and lesbian or bisexual identity. (b) Among men, the relationships among same-sex desire, sexual behaviour with same-sex partners, and gay or bisexual identity.

meanings and interpretations, depending on context and purpose' (Laumann, Gagnon, Michael, & Michaels, 1994: 301).

Framing Sexuality

We have just seen some of the ways in which human sexuality may be defined and measured. But what, conceptually, might the relationships be between masculinity, femininity, heterosexuality, and homosexuality? Scholars generally think about this in one of two possible ways (see Jordan-Young, 2010 for this and the discussion that follows next):

1. Perhaps people are either attracted to men (androphilic) or to women (gynephilic). If this is true, then heterosexual women *and* gay men are both androphilic. Maybe getting at the underlying origins of androphilia could help explain heterosexual desire in women and homosexual desire in men. In this framework, the XY people with cloacal dystrophy discussed in the previous chapter have all turned out to be gynephilic, regardless of their gender identity.
2. Or, maybe homosexuality is just what the word means—attraction to one's own sex—women to women or men to other men. (I am leaving out bisexuality here to simplify the discussion.)

[handwritten in left margin: I don't get it]

In scientific research, frameworks matter. If, as many biologists believe, there is a center in the brain that controls desire, then it might make sense to think of the center as developing in a masculine (prefers females) or a feminine (prefers males) way, possibly depending on fetal hormonal sex. Neuroscientist Simon LeVay espoused this point of view when he measured the size of a specific brain region in gay and straight men and in straight women. He argued that his findings demonstrated that in some brain regions gay men and straight women's brains are more alike (LeVay, 1991). Although attempts to confirm critical aspects of LeVay's findings have produced mixed results, the important point here is to understand his framework, because many scientists conduct research on homosexuality using this basic point of view (Byne, 1997; Byne, Lasco, Kemether, Shinwari, Edgar, Morgello, et al., 2000; Byne, Tobet, Mattiace, Lasco, Kemether, Edgar, et al., 2001).

Many, but not all. If a scientist uses the same-sex attraction framework for homosexuality *and* considers that gay men and women have differently organized brains than straight men and women, then they have to postulate two different models, one for men and one for women. In this example, high androgen exposure during female development is postulated to lead to homosexuality in women but a lack of androgen exposure causes homosexuality in men. Sometimes the researchers themselves do not recognize the distinction between these different frameworks. The result is a complex literature which is difficult to summarize or consistently interpret. Thus, despite extensive research into the biological causes of sexual desire, we know less about the topic than scientists sometimes claim.

It's All in What You Measure

To put it crassly: if you identify yourself as a straight man, how much canoodling on the side (with men) do you have to do before you get counted as gay (even if you deny being gay)? Or if you don't canoodle, what about fantasizing or having erotic dreams about men? These questions analogize to both men and women, gay and straight identified. Most often, these questions return us to Kinsey's Scale. Researchers ask all sorts of questions about behaviors, fantasies, and identity and rate them on Kinsey's Scale of 0–6. But then they have to decide about where to make their cuts. Are Kinsey 0s straight and Kinsey 6s gay and everyone else gets dropped from the study? Or maybe 0s and 1s get lumped together on one end of the scale and 5s and 6s on the other.

Socio-medical scientist Rebecca Jordan-Young was astounded at the variety of definitions used by researchers. In Figure 6.7 I reproduce her table showing nine studies each using different Kinsey-based definitions of homosexuality. This may turn out to be my favorite table of all time because it illustrates so sublimely the difficulty faced by students of nature. Some philosophers of science think that differences in the natural world are continuous or graded. This would mean that scientist-created categories are always somewhat arbitrary. Do we make the cut at 2 and at 5? Do we cut right down the middle? Others believe that there are natural categories that scientists merely identify, or, to use an oft cited

SUBJECTS GROUPED BY KINSEY SCORES

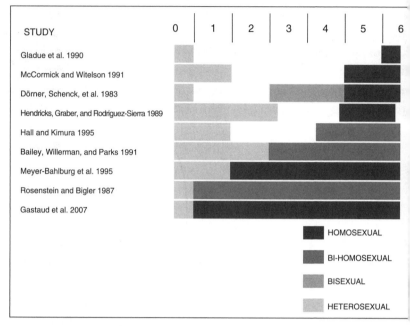

Figure 6.7 Variety in scientists' use of Kinsey Scores. Note that in Meyer-Bahlberg et al. (1995) and Gastaud et al. (2007), the labels are implicit rather than explicit (for example, "subjects with homosexual inclinations" rather than "homosexuals").

metaphor, scientific categories carve nature at her joints. (Think of that holiday turkey. Do you carefully identify where two separate bones are joined by cartilage and carve through the connective tissue? Or do you take a pair of big, old poultry shears and chop through bone wherever it is to make chunks of a size that can fit neatly on a serving platter?)

Jordan-Young believes that researchers who identify their research subjects by prenatal hormone status—for example, people who study variations in sexual development such as Congenital Adrenal Hyperplasia often adopt the continuum approach. In contrast, those who study a general population and group their subjects by sexual orientation are more likely to use strong categories. Each approach is designed to "catch" as much difference as possible. There is nothing wrong with

strong categories are dividing)

#3

this. Scientists design studies with an eye towards maximizing chances of finding something measurable and hopefully of theoretical significance. The problem comes when those same scientists forget that their definitions are conveniences that only partially reflect what exists in the world. Sometimes, for example, researchers may drop a proportion of their subjects because, while they seemed homosexual in some ways, their answers to questionnaires were "inconsistent." In such a case, the act of excluding the sort of multidimensionality seen in Edward Laumann's studies, defines homosexuality as a two-dimensional, absolute state. You either are or you're not.

Scientists who think that biological variation causes or strongly contributes to human homosexuality go for the strong categories. Recent work frames partner choice as one of the most pronounced sex differences we know of. And this is certainly one way to look at it: most men prefer women as partners and most women prefer men (Bocklandt & Vilain, 2007; Ngun, Ghahramani, Sanchez, Bocklandt, & Vilain, 2010). In searching for possible genetic, hormonal, or neurological underpinnings of partner preference, researchers have found samples that at least for men show a bimodal pattern of sexual orientation (Hamer, Hu, Magnuson, Hu, & Pattatucci, 1993), a finding quite different from studies such as Laumann's (Figure 6.6). The big difference between the approaches of geneticists and those of sociologists such as Laumann is how they find their samples. Dean Hamer and his colleagues targeted a specific population by recruiting research subjects at AIDS clinics. Others have found subjects at gay rights parades or gay bars. Laumann and his colleagues find their subjects using more of a dragnet approach. They randomly sample the entire population in a city or neighborhood.

And this is the dilemma. If a geneticist is to have any hope of identifying a gene involved with any kind of trait, he or she has to look for the strongest version of that trait. Also the cost, time, and technical expertise needed to survey an entire population is great; and, when a funder gives money for a genetics study, the donor does not want the first three or four years spent acquiring a giant population sample. They want genes to be isolated and correlations to be found, or not. But by going for samples of convenience, emphasizing the extreme cases, the muddled middle disappears (at least for men).

Let's for the moment grant biologists their bimodal distributions for sexual preference in men. Given their findings for the samples they selected, what have they found out about genes, hormones, the brain, and sexual preference? On the matter of prenatal hormones and sexual orientation, experts hedge their bets. In one recent article the authors find that "there is no convincing evidence linking differences in sexual orientation to variations in prenatal androgen" (Bocklandt & Vilain, 2007: 256), while a second expert supports "a prenatal role for androgen in promoting male-typical sexual orientation" but hastens to add that hormones in the prenatal environment are "not the only factor determining" sexual orientation (Hines, 2009: 1886). Note that the phrase "male-typical sexual orientation" implicitly embraces an androphilic/gynophilic model of sexual orientation.

With regard to possible structural differences in the brains of homosexual vs heterosexual men there are no undisputed positive findings. And even if there were, we would not have information about causation, since when we study adult brains, we can't tell whether the brain developed in response to prior experience or whether the brain anatomy led to particular behavioral patterns. It is the chicken or egg problem all over again.

What a Difference a Sample Makes!

But if not hormones or brains, what about genes? One way to find out if genes influence a particular behavior is to study twin pairs in which either both identify as gay (concordant) or one member identifies as gay and the other doesn't (discordant). Investigators seek out identical twins, because they share 100 percent of their genes, and compare them to so-called fraternal twins, who share half of their genes, just like any regular pair of siblings. If identical twins are both homosexual more often than are fraternal twins, researchers usually conclude that they have measured a genetic contribution to the development of homosexuality. This assumes, of course, that identical twins are treated as differently in the family and in other social networks as are fraternal twins, or that similar treatment ought not to influence this particular behavior. Since we have no idea what "treatments" might affect sexual preference, this is a difficult assumption to test. Even so, the better twin studies make an honest effort to test factors that they can identify and know how to measure.

In the 1990s a number of twin studies appeared that seemed to point toward a strong genetic component to homosexuality. For example, researchers who published in 1991 concluded that "male sexual orientation is substantially genetic." They found that "fifty-two percent of the identical twin brothers were gay, as against 22 percent of non-identical twins and 11 percent of the adoptive, genetically unrelated brothers" (Bailey & Pillard, 1991a, 1991b). Significant criticism of this study stems from the small sample size and the related fact that the subjects were people who answered ads in magazines and newspapers that catered to a gay audience. Could bias based on the method of finding study subjects seriously affect the results? This question bothered the scientists who conducted the study enough that when they had a chance to ask the same questions again with a more neutrally obtained study sample they did so—and the results were quite different.

This time, psychologist J. Michael Bailey and his colleagues obtained their study group from an Australian registry that lists 25,000 twin pairs of all sexualities. This enabled the researchers to whittle down their sample to include both identical and fraternal brothers, sisters, and mixed fraternal twin pairs. Even though there was some self selection (some of the twins failed to participate for unknown reasons) they ended up with a pretty big sample size obtained in a more random fashion than the earlier studies. And it turns out how you find your subjects really matters (Bailey, Dunne, & Martin, 2000).

Previous studies by Bailey and colleagues had found that if one member of an identical twin pair was gay, then about 47–48 percent of the time the second pair member was also gay. But the new report, which had larger samples and avoided ascertainment bias, found that the concordance for twin pairs was only 20 percent for male pairs and 24 percent for female pairs. This suggested, they wrote, "that concordances from prior studies were inflated because of concordance-dependent ascertainment bias" (ibid.: 533). Because Bailey identified a strong link between early childhood gender non-conformity (those boys who loved dolls and those girls who were passionate about rugby) and homosexuality, they examined possible links between gender non-conformity, gender identity, and homosexuality, looking for evidence of both genetic influence and family environmental factors, both of which are considered to be familial traits. Importantly, the word "familial" does not distinguish between family genes and family environment. The results: homosexuality in their sample had strong familial influences, but "it was more difficult to resolve the relative importance of additive genetic and shared environmental factors" (ibid.: 531). Which is to say, they could not provide significant support for the importance of genes to the development of homosexuality. In contrast, they did find evidence of a partial genetic contribution to childhood gender non-conformity. The fact that this genetic contribution is far from absolute and appears to be stronger in males than in females suggests that there is still a lot to be explained by examining the developmental dynamics of desire.

What about DNA?

Let's make this brief. Several molecular biology labs have looked for segments of DNA common to men and women whom they have identified as gay. The results have been mixed—reports that cannot be confirmed, studies that don't reveal much because the sample size is too small, possible problems with ascertainment bias, etc. Beyond any specific study, however, there are several problems inherent to the approach that make it unlikely the search for a DNA sequence or sequences linked to homosexuality will ever pan out.

1. We already know that if there are genes involved, there must be a number of them, each of which has a small effect. This makes it difficult to identify them without using very large population samples, something hard to do, as we have already seen.
2. We already know that environmental factors play an important role in the development of sexual preference. If genes and environment interact, then the effect of a gene might be great in one environment

and small or non-existent in another. So hunting for genes would be best done by comparing people in different environments. But this is hard to do because we really don't know what the relevant environments are.

3. Studying the genetics of behavior is always difficult because some combinations of genes might not be enough for a measurable behavior to emerge (Mustanski, Chivers, & Bailey, 2002).

There is another way.

Framing the Study of Desire

So far I have done nothing but complain about how hard it is to study human sexuality. And it *is* hard. But if scientists were to openly articulate our measurement and framing issues, and our differing theoretical stances, perhaps we could develop a few parallel research programs that, while differing in their points of view, could fruitfully acknowledge one another and, dare I say, rationally cross check findings and regularly rethink theories and frames with subtlety and respect.

Here are the premises *I* would use to frame research on human sexuality:

1. Sexual desire has a neurophysiological component that individuals come to interpret as pleasure and attraction. In other words what we think of as emotions have an underlying physiology.

2. The underlying physiology develops over time as much in response to specific experiences as it is a driver of specific experiences. In other words, sexuality is dynamic *and* "in the body."

3. To study the development of adult sexuality and desire, we need to start by understanding the physiology and embodiment of pleasure from infancy (Freud—are you still there?), through childhood, adolescence, young adulthood, into middle and old age. That is, embodied sexuality and desire at physio-emotional levels has a life cycle. Expression at any stage of the cycle is conditioned in part by what has gone before. How we have trained our bodies in our

pre-teens, teens, and twenties affects how our bodies respond in our thirties and forties.
4. Finally, I would accept the complexity and contextual nature of desire. This is really where a lot of the argument lies. Many scholars (I will call them fundamentalists) treat sexual preference or orientation as a fixed thing—a characteristic, a permanent phenotype; true, an individual might deviate from his or her phenotype for some temporary reason. But the deviation would not alter the fundamental phenotype. Sailors at sea for long periods of time, for example, might have sexual experiences with one another, but only because women were absent. Once on shore leave, those who were fundamentally heterosexual would immediately seek out women for company, those who were homosexual would seek out other men.

Many researchers, especially those interested in the biological aspects of sexuality, fully accept this framework, which is why they have no problem studying only the strong categories. In contrast, sociologists such as Laumann, and some psychologists and anthropologists, think that throwing out the inconsistent or intermediate groups leaves you with watery gruel rather than a rich human porridge. In her book *Sexual Fluidity*, psychologist Lisa Diamond reviews these points of view in a very helpful fashion (Diamond, 2008) (I will call the latter contextualists, or alternatively developmentalists). Let's explore the problem with an historical example.

Alexander Berkman (1870–1936) was a Russian- (today it would be Lithuanian-) born anarchist who emigrated to the United States where he and his more famous lover and political compatriot Emma Goldman (1869–1940) engaged in a form of political activism that included what they called "propaganda of the deed." One such deed was his attempt to assassinate the American industrialist and steel baron, Henry Clay Frick (1849–1919). This act landed Berkman in jail, where he served 14 years of a 22 year sentence. Which brings us to his *Prison Memoirs of an Anarchist*, which contains some amazingly explicit (for the time) passages about love, emotions, and sex in the prison (Berkman, 1912). It is these I want to examine.

On the one hand, Berkman's heterosexual passions were strong. He pined for Goldman and other lovers and wrote movingly of his young love and passion. On the other, there is no doubt that in prison he fell in love, it seems at least twice, with other men. This happened in a context of great loneliness (he was in solitary for long periods of time), but the passion was real. Consider the following passage describing his interchanges with another prisoner called Johnny:

> we converse ... talking in a frank, confidential manner. With a glow of pleasure, I become aware of the note of tenderness in his voice ... the springs of affection well up within me, as I lie huddled on the stone floor ... With closed eyes, I picture the boy before me, with his delicate face, and sensitive girlish lips ... [In a later conversation, Berkman reports the following exchange] Johnny says "if you were here with me I would like to kiss you." [Berkman writes] An unaccountable sense of joy glows in my heart ... [I reply] I feel just as you do ...
>
> (ibid.: 322–323)

This passage is an easy one for the fundamentalists. They readily acknowledge that a heterosexual man can fall in love in an extreme setting such as prison. But because they "revert" to their heterosexuality (as Berkman did) when they return to mixed company, a fundamentalist would say that heterosexuality remains the essential phenotype of a man such as Berkman. Rather than focus on an enduring essence, however, a contextualist would emphasize the diverse capacities of sexual desire and expression found within any one individual. For a contextualist, what is most interesting is the developmental dynamic that allows a set of feelings and desires to stabilize under a certain set of conditions. Equally interesting for these scholars are the conditions that destabilize one form of sexual desire and allow new forms to emerge and stabilize.

Perhaps even more telling for the contextualist is a story Berkman tells late in the book about a conversation with a fellow prisoner called George. In this frank conversation they discuss everything from masturbation to pederasty, but what finally emerges is George's gradual transformation from a married, heterosexual man who held strong prejudices against homosexuals, to a man who, in prison, fell deeply in love with another prisoner and did not "revert back" to heterosexual engagements. "It came very gradually," he wrote of his falling in love. "For two years I loved him without the least taint of sex desire ... But by degrees the psychic state began to manifest all the expressions of love between the opposite sexes ... Perhaps you will smile at this Aleck but it was real, true love ..." (ibid.: 438–439).

If the above passage had been written by a woman rather than a man most modern-day sexologists would not even blink. There is a growing consensus that men and women differ rather dramatically in how their sexual orientation and desire manifests itself over the life cycle. This is why the speaker at the meeting on sex and gender whom I quoted earlier (men straightforward, women complex) said what he said. When pushed, even the fundamentalists, who will argue fiercely that men are either gay or straight and pretty much begin life that way and remain so until death, will agree that their theories don't really work for women. Some fundamentalists argue, in fact, that in contrast to men, women don't "have" a sexual orientation, if by the latter one means a permanent, usually unchangeable preference for sexual and love partners of the same sex.

Psychologist Lisa Diamond has supplied strong evidence for this point of view. Recently, she reported on the first ten years of a life cycle study of sexual preference in women who initially identified themselves as having a same sex orientation. Diamond recruited her sample of about 100 women when they were young—average age of 20—and has interviewed them every two years since then. Each time she assessed their place on a Kinsey Scale, and also asked directly how their sexuality has changed (or not) and how they conceptualize their own identity compared to their previous interview. Since this is an ongoing study, we can expect more to emerge as "her women" move from their teens and twenties into middle age and beyond. Her early findings are tantalizing (Diamond, 2008).

To start with her sample consisted of 43 percent self-identified lesbians, 30 percent self-identified bisexuals and 27 percent who, while considering themselves to be "non-heterosexual" did not otherwise label themselves. Diamond was surprised to discover that a mere two years after her first interview about one third of the women had changed their identities. And the types of switching did not fit current theories. Some changed from un-labeled to lesbian or bisexual; others switched from lesbian or bisexual to un-labeled; and a third group switched from lesbian to heterosexual. Well, Diamond reasoned, these women are all young; perhaps their sexual identity development is still in flux; surely they will have settled down by the time of the next couple of interviews. *Not!*

Over the course of ten years the women continued to switch categories "typically in a way that broadened, rather than narrowed their potential range of attractions and relationships" (ibid.: 67). Astoundingly, in ten years two thirds of the women had changed their sexual identity labels at least once (Diamond, 2007). As a result of her findings, Diamond identifies four important aspects of female sexuality. First, she concludes that women *do* have a general sexual orientation, most commonly to men, but also to both sexes and, less frequently, mainly to other women. Second, Diamond suggests that in addition to a general sexual orientation women are sensitive to situations and relationships that might mediate erotic feelings. She calls this "sexual fluidity" and offers as examples intense emotional relationships or greater positive exposure to same-sex relationships. Third, fluidity can trigger sexual attractions that may be short or long-lived. Fourth, just as women have different orientations, not all women are equally fluid. This means that the same "trigger experiences" might trigger fluidity in one person but not another.

How different is Diamond's picture of female sexuality from what we know about male sexuality and why? First, the differences may be matters of degree rather than kind. Alexander Berkman's sexual fluidity appeared under circumstances of extreme deprivation, but it does seem fair to describe the incidents in his prison memoir as fluidity. Perhaps men also have the trait of sexual fluidity, but it is less easily evoked than for women. If so, why might that be? Here we return to the frustration of inadequate theory. We simply do not understand either the biological or the psychological, sociological, and cultural processes by which human sexual desire develops. It is not surprising that the developmental pathways seem to differ in men and women. The sexes differ with regard to physiological and reproductive development. But so too do they differ with regard to psychological, sociological, and cultural development, so sorting out the one from the other is pretty difficult.

Indeed, the future understandings of human sexuality lie in our ability to design dynamic, multidimensional approaches that can follow the development of sexual desire, orientation, and fluidity throughout the life cycle. Diamond has already begun to place her first decade of findings on women in a new theoretical context. For example, she documents non-linear discontinuities rather than linear and continuous changes in female sexual expression. She notes that, for women, new forms of sexual expression seem to self organize and emerge rather suddenly in new contexts, but that each new state can remain stable over relatively long periods of time. These are the hallmarks of a dynamic system and they may well apply to men, although the time scale of change, the strength of stable states, and the extremity of altered contexts which lead to change will very likely be found to differ.

Further Reading

Ansermet, F., Magistretti, P., & Fairfield, S. (2007). *Biology of Freedom: Neural Plasticity, Experience and the Unconscious.* New York: Other Press.

Bailey, J. M., & Zucker, K. (1995). Childhood sex-typed behavior and sexual orientation: A conceptual analysis and quantitative review. *Developmental Psychology,* 31(1), 43–55.

D'Emilio, J., & Freedman, E. B. (1988). *Intimate Matters: A History of Sexuality in America.* New York: Harper and Row.

Ellis, H. (1913). *Studies in the Psychology of Sex.* Philadelphia, PA: P.A. Davis.

Harris, A. (2005). *Gender as Soft Assembly.* Hillsdale, NJ: The Analytic Press.

Katz, J. N. (1995). *The Invention of Heterosexuality.* New York: Dutton.

Krafft-Ebing, R. V. (1892). *Psychopathia Sexualis, with Especial Reference to Contrary Sexual Instinct: A Medico-Legal Study.* Philadelphia, PA: F.A. Davis.

Nye, R. A. (Ed.) (1998). *Sexuality.* Oxford: Oxford University Press.

Stein, E. (1999). *The Mismeasure of Desire: The Science, Theory and Ethics of Sexual Orientation.* Oxford: Oxford University Press.

7

THINKING ABOUT GROUPS;
THINKING ABOUT INDIVIDUALS

Difference in Context

Boys and girls have a lot in common but they also differ. They begin their developmental journeys with different chromosomes, but at first have identical gonads, and internal and external genitals. Hormone levels that orchestrate portions of sexual development differ as well. As development proceeds these "bits and pieces" diverge. In societies in which food is varied and plentiful and pregnant women well fed, we find a number of average differences between boys and girls at birth. How do we best interpret these differences? Does gender necessarily predict the future of each individual as he or she appears on earth? At one level this question might seem simple—the answer is *yes*. Gender matters. (To follow up on this point check out the field of feminist geography (Seager, 2003).) At other levels, however, the answer is not so obvious, a claim we explore in the next few pages.

Let's start with brain or head size, where head circumference is usually seen as a valid stand in for brain size. A summary of studies of head size in developing fetuses and in neonates reveals a couple of noteworthy results (Table 7.1). First, most studies have been done on infants born in relatively wealthy, industrialized countries. The importance of this fact will become clear in a moment. Second, the size of the differences have been measured using a special statistic called Cohen's d.

Table 7.1 Sex differences in biparietal diameter and head circumference

Study	Sample	N	Measures	Girls' mean	Boys' mean	Cohen's d
(Bromley, Frigoletto, Harlow, Evans, & Benacerraf, 1993)	Healthy fetuses at 18 g.w.	1247	Biparietal diameter	42.1 mm	**42.8 mm**	.30
	Healthy fetuses at 19 g.w.	2089		44.8 mm	**45.7 mm**	.37
	Healthy fetuses at 20 g.w.	1635		47.8 mm	**48.7 mm**	.37
	Healthy fetuses at 21 g.w.	694		50.6 mm	**51.3 mm**	.27
(Crawford, Doyle, & Meadows, 1987)	Healthy neonates in London	99	Head circumference	33.8 cm	**34.6 cm**	.39

Scientists calculate Cohen's d by subtracting the difference between the means of two populations and then dividing by a statistic called the standard deviation. This number measures how variable each population is. In one study in Table 7.1 for example, the mean for girls' head circumference was 33.8 cm and for boys' was 34.6 cm (Crawford, Doyle, & Meadows, 1987). The Cohen's d was 0.39, which means that 73 percent of boys and girls overlap for brain size at birth (Figure 7.1).

In a different study of brain diameter at 21 weeks of gestation, a smaller difference was found. In this case the Cohen's d was 0.27, an overlap of about 80 percent (Bromley, Frigoletto, Harlow, Evans, & Benacerraf, 1993). Most psychologists consider these to be small differences (compared to, say, the difference between chihuahuas and Saint Bernards in Figure 4.3). A sex difference in brain size is also seen in

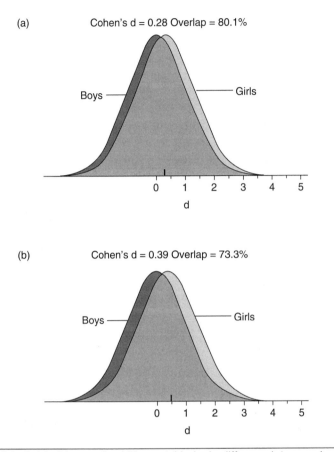

Figure 7.1 Cohen's d for (a) prenatal and (b) neonatal brain size differences between males and females.

For a color version of this figure please go to www.routledge.com/cw/fausto-sterling

older children and adults but there is a gap in information about size differences between birth and 4 years of age (Giedd, Castellanos, Rajapakse, Vaituzis, & Rapoport, 1997). Since the first four years involve enormous changes in brain size and complexity, we can't understand later size differences without studying this period of great growth. A lot could be going on. The initial size differences could increase or disappear. New differences could take shape. And these might depend on different types and quantities of neural stimulation, or different maternal diets all of which could induce different genetic activities during gestation. Furthermore, the fact that the differences involved are so small means that the brain size of most boys and girls are not different at all (Figure 7.1). In other words, even though there is an average or mean difference between the group we call boys and the group we call girls (that would be an average group difference), we cannot infer the brain size of any individual based on knowing merely that they are a boy or a girl.

Before considering why any of this might matter later in life, let's look at a second example and tuck one more important concept—the norm of reaction—under our belt. At birth (in countries with good maternal nutrition) boys outweigh girls by almost half a pound (effect sizes of 0.15 to 0.40, i.e. 73 to 89 percent overlap in male and female birth populations) (Australian Institute of Health and Welfare, 2000; Crawford et al., 1987; Davis, Cutter, Goldenberg, Hoffman, Cliver, & Brumfield, 1993; CDC growth charts 2000), although the weight differences disappear by ages 2–3 years.

Now let's make this story a little more complicated. How, for example, do relative birthweights vary when nutrition is better or worse, or mothers are more likely to be ill? An analysis from the World Health Organization of a large body of published studies found that the male-female difference in birth weight in developed countries was about three tenths of a pound. However, the sex difference in developing nations was only two tenths of a pound (Kramer, 1987). What does this comparison between developed and developing countries tell us? First off, we know that birth weight increases with better nutrition and health and that overall birth weight has increased a great deal in developed countries over the past few decades. But when birth weight is low or when it is high, are boys and girls equally affected? Do XX and XY embryos respond to the same degree to low and to high nutrition, to certain types of illness, or to maternal smoking or other known factors affecting birth weight? It turns out that such information is hard to find.

In the language of geneticists what I am really asking is: do XX and XY embryos have the same *norm of reaction* for each of a number of environmental situations? A norm of reaction? What is *that*? Well for one thing, it is a concept that most people who do huge population studies of birth weight seem unaware of. As an example, consider the insect eye, or more specifically the beady-eyed little fruit fly. The beads in that beady little eye are individual light receiving organs called ommatidia, and the overall size of the eye depends on the number of ommatidia. This number depends, in turn, on many things including the temperature at which the fly developed and the genetic make-up of each fly. We can see this clearly in Figure 7.2 which shows the norm of reaction for fly eye development under different growth temperatures. Particularly interesting are the two mutants, which have opposite responses to temperature. At lower temperatures they look identical and at higher temperatures they differ vastly. Norms of reaction can be measured for any environmental trait of interest. In the case of the plant genus *Ranunculus*, leaf shape depends on whether the plant grows underwater, at the water–air interface, or in *plein air*. One important point—there is no way to intuit a norm of reaction. It must be measured, rather than imagined or taken for granted.

Now consider a report from a Canadian epidemiologist that between 1981 and 2003 the mean birth weight for Canadian girls has increased at a faster rate than for boys. This means that the sex difference in birth weights has gotten smaller. This contrasts with a comparison between developing and developed countries, since boys have gotten relatively larger in wealthier nations. The intriguing question is why (van Vliet, Liu, & Kramer, 2009). The report's authors hypothesize that the decreasing difference is abnormal and might be due to pollution from substances that disrupt androgen function. Although evidence is scarce, they could be right. The future of gender may well be affected by these endocrine disrupting pollutants. But there is a less ominous possibility as well, just waiting to be carefully tested.

Suppose that XX and XY fetuses differ in their norms of reaction for improved nutrition, decreased maternal smoking, or other factors that increase fetal growth and birth weight. Canada is, after all, a nation which has taken great strides in optimizing health. Maybe, at the very high end of the gestational health spectrum, XX and XY fetuses just aren't that different. What we could be witnessing, then, is the disappearance of a well established biological sex difference. The reason might

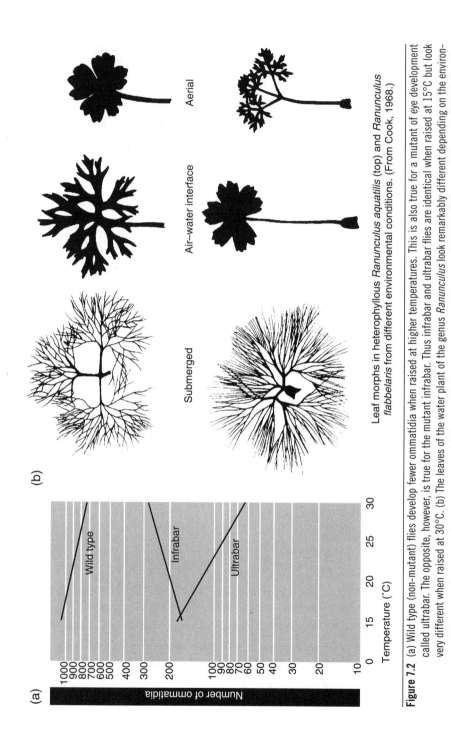

Figure 7.2 (a) Wild type (non-mutant) flies develop fewer ommatidia when raised at higher temperatures. This is also true for a mutant of eye development called ultrabar. The opposite, however, is true for the mutant infrabar. Thus infrabar and ultrabar flies are identical when raised at 15°C but look very different when raised at 30°C. (b) The leaves of the water plant of the genus *Ranunculus* look remarkably different depending on the environ-

Leaf morphs in heterophyllous *Ranunculus aquatilis* (top) and *Ranunculus flabbelaris* from different environmental conditions. (From Cook, 1968.)

be nefarious (anti-androgen pollution) but it might be the end result of a culture that has vastly improved maternal health and nutrition. I have scoured the literature on birth weight to see if I could find evidence for the latter explanation and aside from the 1987 WHO study already cited, there is nothing to be found. Indeed the concept of a norm of reaction does not seem to be in use among scientists who study sex differences in birth weight, so on this point, the future of gender is still to be written.

Does Any of This Matter for Adults?

O.K. We have these differences at birth. They are small; they don't tell us much about any particular individual. And they may be a moving target as the environmental conditions for fetal growth and development change. Do they really matter at all? We can visit this question by jumping ahead and asking (1) what do we know about sex differences in adults? and (2) if there are any, where they might have come from?

If there *are* any? But of course there are. We know that men are from Mars and women are from Venus. We read about it all the time in the media. Well, "not so fast" says psychologist Janet Hyde. In 2005 Hyde published her Gender Similarities Hypothesis. She started by surveying all the studies of sex differences in adolescents and adults that she could find. She pooled and analyzed the data from these many reports (Table 7.2) in order to estimate just how large these differences were. On the whole, the size of each published difference was small (using Cohen's d as a measure). The exceptions were throwing velocity, physical aggression, and attitudes about casual sex. The other differences were small and possibly continuing to decrease in size (Hyde, 2005, 2007; Hyde, Lindberg, Linn, Ellis, & Williams, 2008).

When possible, Hyde broke down her findings by age. For example, studies of the ability to solve complex math problems showed no sex-related differences from ages 5 to 10, tiny differences in the early teens, and growing differences in the late teens and early twenties. The largest effect size was 0.32 (or 76 percent overlap). Differences do not always increase with age however. Hyde reported that sex-related differences in self esteem increased through late adolescence but then decreased to

Table 7.2 A sample of effect sizes extracted from 46 meta-analyses of research on psychological gender differences

Variable	No. of reports	Effect size (d)
Cognitive variables		
Mathematics problem solving	48	+0.08
Mathematics	6*	+0.16
Reading comprehension	5*	−0.09
Mental rotation	78	+0.56
Communication		
Self-disclosure	205	−0.18
Smiling	418	−0.40
Social and personality variables		
Physical aggression	111	+0.33 to +0.84
Verbal aggression	68	+0.09 to +0.55
Helping behavior	99	+0.13
Leadership effectiveness	76	−0.02
Self-esteem	216	+0.21
Depression symptoms	49	−0.16
Attitudes about casual sex	10	+0.81
Miscellaneous		
Throwing velocity	12	+2.18
Moral reasoning: justice orientation	95	+.019

Source: Hyde (2005)
* Data were from major, national samples

virtually zero in adults. Once again, the important point is developmental. The math difference did not exist in young children, began to grow during the teen years and became larger in young adulthood. Knowing the developmental dynamics of a trait allows researchers to look at the emergence or disappearance of difference, asking what components of each individual's being and experience contribute to its growth and maintenance.

Not only do many sex-related differences that exist in adulthood develop over the course of individual development, but the aggregate trends can change over time. This latter fact also gives us insight into the stream of experience contributing to specific skill development and again suggests that difference is not usually static. Rather it is a steady state supported by a particular developmental history, time, and place. For example, data from the 1970s and 1980s showed a 25 percent deficit in complex problem solving for girls compared to boys, starting in high school. Measurements made from standardized tests in the last decade, however, suggest that these differences have almost evaporated. Why? Hyde points to one important factor: before the year 2000 girls took fewer advanced high school math and science courses than boys. Today, they study high school calculus at the same rate as boys and earn 48 percent of the undergraduate mathematics degrees (Hyde et al., 2008).

Hyde reported on still other studies in which the size and even the direction of sex-related differences varied with context. For example experimenters tested college students with similar math training. In one condition they told students that men had in the past done better than women on the test. In another they said the test was "gender fair." In the first case women did more poorly than men, while in the second condition there were no sex differences. "The conclusion," Hyde writes, "is clear." The size and "even the direction of gender differences depends on the context" (2005: 589). Hyde argues that this fact, the fact that differences develop rather than appear full blown, and that most differences are small argues against a "men are from Mars, women are from Venus" differences model, with its idea that psychological sex-related differences are large and stable (Hyde, 2005).

Not everyone accepts Hyde's ideas. Psychologist Richard Lippa has several objections. He points, for example, to a report of large differences in women's and men's occupational preferences as well as noting childhood differences in toy preferences and play styles. Still, Lippa's "the gender reality hypothesis" actually sounds quite similar to Hyde's "sex similarities." Lippa holds that many differences are small, some are intermediate, and a few are large (Lippa, 2006). Both Lippa and Hyde agree on one central idea, however: the task that still confronts scientists is to understand more about the mechanisms which produce both similarities and differences. Why do they appear and disappear? Why are some stable and others highly context dependent? We have no clear answers to these questions, but in the next chapter we offer some new ways to analyze the problem.

Further Reading

Center for Disease Control (2000). 2000 CDC growth charts: United States. Retrieved from: http://www.cdc.gov/growthcharts, accessed December 13, 2011.

Gilbert, S. F., & Epel, D. (2008). *Ecological Developmental Biology*. Sunderland, MA: Sinauer Associates.

Krimsky, Sheldon (2002). *Hormonal Chaos: The Scientific and Social Origins of the Environmental Endocrine Hypothesis*. Baltimore, MD: Johns Hopkins University Press.

Lewontin, R. (1982). *Human Diversity*. New York: Scientific American Books.

Schlichting, C. D., & Pigliucci, M. (1998). *Phenotypic Evolution: A Reaction Norm Perspective*. Sunderland, MA: Sinauer Associates.

Seager, J. (2003). *The Penguin Atlas of Women in the World*. London: Myriad Editions.

Steele, Claude (2010). *Whistling Vivaldi: And Other Clues to how Stereotypes Affect Us*. New York: W.W. Norton.

Defining what color is

girls boys

8
PINK AND BLUE FOREVER

Interlude

Let's think about baby blankets and infant clothing. Start by looking at websites that sell baby clothes, for example, http://www.carters.com. First, note the sex segregation. If you go to the girls' side (listed in a pink font) you can buy that special newborn baby girl a pink monkey or a pink butterfly sleep and play outfit. Or maybe you would like to get her a pink puppy, long sleeved tee shirt, or a tee with a silver horse on a bright pink background. You get the idea. But if you click on the blue font list for boys you get other choices: a blue car, cotton sleep outfit, a rough and tough, orange thermal tee shirt, a grey and blue goal kicker tee, or a sporty handsome cotton sleep and play that looks like a baby version of a professional baseball outfit. There is no mistaking which baby is the boy and which the girl, right? Just look at the blanket color or what they are wearing. And why not? From time immemorial haven't adults dressed their little boys and little girls differently? Haven't adults always wanted to be able to tell at a glance whether the infant before them is a boy or a girl? Well, it turns out, not so much.

Our current obsession with baby sex seems to have started in about 1920. At the same time that we developed the need to know at a glance whether an infant was a boy or a girl, we also did a 180 on the pink and blue thing. Consider an article written in 1914 in a US newspaper called

defining girl & boy

boy & girl

the *Sunday Sentinel.* "If you like the color note on the little one's garments," the report advised mothers, "use pink for the boy and blue for the girl." A 1918 piece in the *Ladies Home Journal* opined that pink was for boys and blue for girls because pink is "a more decided and stronger color . . . more suitable for the boy, while blue . . . is more delicate and dainty . . . prettier for the girl" (cited in Frassanito & Pettorini, 2008: 881). As recently as 1940 red and pink symbolized strength and courage and blue faith and constancy. Catholic traditions in Europe associated blue with the Virgin Mary; but by the 1930s Nazi Germany, especially via the pink triangle used to stigmatize homosexual men, anchored a new association of pink with femininity (Frassanito & Pettorini, 2008). After World War II the reversal seemed complete. Military uniforms were made out of blue cloth and the association with masculinity in the United States and Western Europe was fixed, but recently enough that the generation of adults currently in their fifties was the first to be brought up with strict pink=female, blue=male color coding (Paoletti, 1997).

The color switch was part of a bigger transformation in children's clothing style. In the late 1880s all infants were dressed in long white dresses until they started to walk. As toddlers both boys and girls wore short, loose-fitting dresses, and from 3 to about 5 years all kids wore dresses or suits with short skirts. Boys and girls wore slightly different outfits, but basically their dress most nearly resembled women's clothing. In this period adults seemed more preoccupied with dress that distinguished between children and adults than boys from girls. Why this began to change is uncertain. One can, however, speculate that as adult women entered the public sphere, as they attained civil rights such as the vote and the right to own property, that clarifying gender boundaries for babies and children grew more important (Paoletti, 1987). Whatever the reason, at the end of the 1890s by age 2 or 3 little boys stopped wearing dresses. This change met with some resistance, especially from feminists. In 1910 feminist Charlotte Perkins Gilman wrote of the "conspicuous evil" of a "premature and unnatural differentiation in sex in the dress of little children" (cited in Paoletti, 1987: 142). But the tide of early gender differentiation did not turn back.

I have walked us through this interlude for two reasons. First, sometimes things that seem obvious, universal, and unchangeable really aren't.
Strong as it is, the specific shape of so-called feminine and masculine
color coding is peculiar to our (historical) period. Pink and blue provide
a colorful example of socially produced gender coding. Second, despite
the code being socially produced, it probably *has* changed how our bodies
work. This leads me to the last section of the book—understanding sex
and gender as a developmental dynamic in which the social, the cultural,
and the body are so intertwined that if we try to disentangle them we
end up losing the forest amidst the trees. To explain this, let's further
explore pink and blue and toys for boys (and girls).

Feel
color represents
what you're feeling

Kids develop strong color pre-

based on environment show children preference on color

9

THE DEVELOPMENTAL DYNAMICS OF PINK AND BLUE

Developing Color Preferences

Korean artist JeongMee Yoon is obsessed with pink and blue. Or rather her young daughter was obsessed with pink, which led Yoon to produce photos such as "Lauren and Carolyn and Their Pink Things" and "Ethan and His Blue Things" which depict infants surrounded by a sea of blue or a sea of pink objects. Yoon's daughter is far from the only little girl in love with the color pink (Figure 2.3). Parenting blogs provide anecdotal evidence that children over the age of 1 year sometimes develop strong color preferences. One parent asks if it is normal for her 16 month old son to be obsessed with the color light green. Another parent replied that his or her daughter had been obsessed since about the same age with hot pink, while a nephew in the same age range had progressed from loving green to a new favorite at age 3.5 of yellow. Others on this blog chimed in: a toddler son who loved orange and then "graduated to black, silver and brown"; a daughter who preferred purple and yellow and whose mother felt she had trained her in the preference by furnishing her from birth with lilac and yellow blankets, clothes, and stuffed animals.[1]

There are few systematic studies of color preference in children under the age of 2. But a study of kids aged 4–11 revealed that more boys than girls liked the colors black, blue, brown, green, and white, while more girls than boys went for pink and purple. Preference, however, was not symmetrical. Boys in this study very rarely chose pink over blue, while girls, although preferring pink on average, chose blue with some frequency. Indeed this is typical of many sex-stereotyped characteristics: boys cling more rigidly to the stereotype than do girls (Chiu, Gervan, Fairbrother, Johnson, Owen-Anderson, Bradley, et al., 2006). How do such preferences develop? The old way of looking at the question is to ask is it nature or is it nurture? Do girls love pink because of something inborn about their visual system? Indeed, is pink-loving an expression of brain sex (Alexander, 2003)? Or, maybe boys choose blue because these days we associate blue with masculinity; maybe adults and peers offer negative feedback to boys who go for pink? I think that this way of approaching the problem is flat out wrong. To use an analogy taken from a recent book on the topic written by historian and philosopher of science Evelyn Fox Keller, imagine the trait "I love pink" as a 100 gallon bucket of water. Suppose two people (oh call one Mr. Nature and the other Ms. Nurture) are filling up that bucket with separate hoses. If Mr. Nature added 70 gallons and Ms. Nurture 30, then we could say that the 100 gallons is due 70 percent to nature and 30 percent to nurture. But suppose instead that Mr. Nature supplies the hose, while Ms. Nurture brings the bucket. Then what percentage is due to nature and what to nurture? The truth is, the question doesn't make any sense (Keller, 2010).

There are better ways to look at this problem. They have different names—dynamic systems, developmental dynamics, developmental systems. But they share a few important features. First, they are developmental; that is to say they examine how a trait comes into being over time. How does a trait *develop*? Second, they ground themselves in the body—not a fixed body—but one that changes over time. This means that to study a trait one always looks at a set of processes over time. Traits may be fairly stable. But if a trait changes—for example, little girls' pink preferences often change into preferences for purple or red—it doesn't start from scratch. Rather new traits build on what is already there. There are other principles to this dynamic approach which the reader may want to look at in more depth, but for now, let's use these ideas to think more deeply about pink and blue.

Training the Nervous System to See

To prefer a color, one must be able to see it. Newborns cannot see all that well. Since the retina of the eye requires light to make all the right nervous connections to the brain, thus insuring mature vision, light exposure after making it down the birth canal is critical for complete development of the nervous system. Neuroscientists say that the region of the brain that translates electrical signals from the retina of the eye into images that we can interpret cannot complete development without extrinsic input (that is light from the environment). Thought about more generally, when light travels through the eyes of newborns, it changes the brain's wiring diagram (Stiles, 2008).

If light matters for the development of vision, maybe newborns that spend a lot of time in a pink environment develop better pink detecting eye-to-brain wiring than children surrounded by blue. If this were the case, it would be a great example of a cultural conceit that literally shapes little infant bodies in gender specific ways. Maybe. But to see if this might be the case, we need to examine the development of color vision. Cone cells in the retina—specialized nerve cells which come in three varieties—facilitate color vision. L cones respond best to long wavelength light (on the yellowish side of green); M cones respond best to medium light (on the bluish side of green); while S cones respond best to short wavelength or bluish light. When light hits the retina it initiates biochemical changes in the cone cells which are ultimately translated into an electrical signal that travels through the optic nerve and from there to visual centers in the brain. The full spectral range of color vision requires fine tuning and interpretation by a variety of cells within the brain itself.

Scientists remain uncertain about how color vision develops. Aspects of the ability to detect color are probably fixed before birth; but at least some degree of visual experience is needed to tune the nervous system so that it can perceive a full range of colors (Dobkins, Bosworth, & McCleery, 2009). Amazingly, this "trainability" persists in adulthood, especially for the L-M (red-green) color system. So at least in theory it is possible that exposure to lots of pink or lots of blue could improve perception of one or the other of these color groups (Neitz, Carroll,

Yamauchi, Neitz, & Williams, 2002; Sugita, 2004), although current facts seem to mitigate against this hypothesis. Newborns can distinguish green, yellow, and red from a white background, but the saturation levels of these colors have to be very high—much higher than for adults. The yellow/blue detection systems may take a little longer (a couple of months) to develop than the red/green systems. Researchers speculate that poor color detection in newborns results from an overall immaturity of the eye, cone reception, and brain color interpretation systems (Adams & Courage, 1998; Crognale, Kelly, Weiss, & Teller, 1998; Franklin & Davies, 2004; Teller, 1998)

If early exposure to lots of pink or lots of blue conditions the infant visual system to the point where a physiological preference develops, then the effect is much delayed. Neither 4, 6, or 9 month old boys or girls particularly care for pink; rather, both like blue and red (Franklin, Bevis, Ling, & Hurlbert, 2010; Franklin & Davies, 2004). One and two year old boys and girls both prefer red to pink or strong blue to pale blue (Jadva, Hines, & Golombok, 2010). Still—and despite a perceptual bias *against* pink—by the time they start to talk and make active choices, many girls go for the pink (Chiu et al., 2006). In sum, whatever happens to produce strong preferences takes shape between the second and third year of development, a period when gender self knowledge and an understanding of social expectations are already under active construction.

A Pleasure Principle?

For some children the preference is strong, almost to the point of obsession. And based on current evidence, it doesn't seem to come, developmentally, from the visual nervous system. How, then, does it develop? And just what is a preference anyway? At this point we have to move into the realm of speculation. If truth be told, scientists who study sex differences in color or toy preference have simply not debated what preference might be at the neurobiological level. So here's a thought. Take it. Leave it. Dispute it, or run some experiments designed to test it. But start by talking with and observing some 3 or 4 year old girls. Listen to the delight and pleasure in their voices, watch the excitement in their actions, as they discuss the color pink. Observe the love; soak in the pleasure.

Pleasure? If something pleases us once, we seek it out again. We come to prefer it. Biologists know quite a lot about how the brain develops circuits that cause repeated seeking of the same pleasure. These circuits can help us repeatedly search out things that are good for us; they can also cause addictions to things that ultimately are terribly bad for us. Now love of the color pink never hurt anyone, but the same molecule that leads some adults to become addicted to harmful drugs, might just be involved in causing some girls to seek out all things pink. Yes, dear readers, we are talking about dopamine, a chemical made in the human midbrain by nerve cells with a reputation for strongly responding to rewards. Under some circumstances dopamine neurons may also incite aversive responses to non-rewarding situations (Bromberg-Martin, Matsumoto, & Hikosaka, 2010).

A psychological reward reinforces a behavior and repeated rewards intensify the behavior. Fundamental reward systems include food, physical comfort, sex, and emotional well-being. Secondary systems can include money, beauty, music, and—dare I suggest for some female toddlers—surrounding oneself with lots of pink things. We don't know why pink becomes a stimulus for the brain's reward system, why it becomes linked physiologically to pleasurable feelings. But we can imagine some plausible hypotheses.

First, familiarity may not breed contempt. On the contrary it can offer security and comfort. A toddler who has grown from infancy surrounded primarily by one color may find that he or she takes pleasure in the continued predictability of the environment. Then too, there is the excitement and emotional reward given by adults as they offer toys or admire clothing. Just picture taking a little girl for a stroll dressed in something pink and frilly. Mother may admire her as she is dressing her, but so too will complete strangers stop to ooh and aah. They may also comment on how adorable her little pink doll or stuffed animal is. Each of these positive responses might stimulate the child's dopamine system, causing her to continue to seek out pink things. A preference for pink is not born. It develops.

But what about the boys? Most boys avoid pink but like blue, green, and other darker colors, although not usually with the same passion girls have for pink. To explain this lack of symmetry, I suggest that a second function of the dopamine system comes into play—so-called aversive conditioning (Bromberg-Martin et al., 2010). It is not so much that little boys develop a pleasure in and a passion for blue as it is that they try to avoid pink. Color preference develops during the second or third year, a period when a lot of gender-related development also locks into place. Well before the age of 3, little boys and little girls can identify some gender-typical activities (men carry hammers, women put on make-up). And they have begun the several year process of clarifying their own gender identity. By 3 years, for example, they can correctly respond to the question, "Are you a boy or a girl?" and their gender identity becomes more sophisticated in the following year. So it is not hard to imagine that both praise and criticism related to the propriety of clothing and toy color might be especially salient in this time period. Children develop pride and pleasure in their own competence, including becoming competent at being a "strong little boy" or a "pretty little girl." As with many aspects of gender, it takes larger transgressions for girls to receive negative feedback than it does for boys. Girls, after all, wear jeans and overalls—even blue ones—as well as frilly dresses. Boys, however, have no such latitude. It does not take long for the negativity, the aversive training to come the way of a toddler boy wearing a pink frilly dress.

If I am correct that the dopamine reward and punishment systems lie at the heart of toddler color preference, one question pretty quickly comes to mind. Why doesn't the system work for all children? What accounts for all of the individual variability—from some little boys who prefer pink and frilly (at one end of the spectrum) to little girls who prefer reds or blues, to children who really don't have strong color preferences? Here again we look to developmental systems. To address the problem of individual variability we need more information—information about variations in physical environment, in gender development, in caregiver and peer interactions and attitudes, and in each individual's physiology (Kegel, Bus, & van Ijzendoorn, 2011). To gather this missing information we have to do studies that follow individual children over extended periods of time, charting the several systems we hypothesize contribute to color preference and identifying stable preference outcomes. Everything from the color of the nursery wallpaper, the rods and cones in the retina, color processing in the brain, the behaviors of parents and others, the timing of gender knowledge and identity development, and individual differences in the molecules important in the dopamine systems contribute to a little girl's delight in or a little boy's aversion to the color pink.

[handwritten left margin: colors influencing our decision]

Further Reading

Camazine, S., Deneuborg, J.-L., Franks, N. R., Sneyd, J., Theraulaz, G., & Bonabeau, E (2001). *Self-Organization in Biological Systems.* Princeton, NJ: Princeton University Press.

Gottlieb, G. (1997). *Synthesizing Nature-Nurture: Prenatal Roots of Instinctive Behavior* Mahwah, NJ: Lawrence Erlbaum.

Harris, A. (2005). *Gender as Soft Assembly.* Hillsdale, NJ: The Analytic Press.

Oyama, S. (2000). *The Ontogeny of Information: Developmental Systems and Evolution.* Durham NC: Duke University Press.

Thelen, E., & Smith, L. B. (1994). *A Dynamic Systems Approach to the Development of Cognition and Action.* Cambridge, MA: MIT Press.

Thelen, E., & Ulrich, B. D. (1991). Hidden skills: a dynamic systems analysis of treadmill stepping during the first year. *Monographs in Social Research in Child Development,* 56(1) 1–98; discussion 99–104.

[handwritten notes]

① color influence

② parent Influence

③ How the eye develop through time

④ boys' don't worry to much about color more than girls

10

EPILOGUE: THE FUTURE OF GENDER (AND SEX)

Intro to development (human creation)

Genes, Chromosomes, and Reproductive Systems Change on an Evolutionary Timescale

The development of sex and gender in humans is layered. And so too must be any answer about the future. Take all those sexes—chromosomal, fetal hormonal, anatomical—that develop *in utero*. While it is possible that the human method for developing these sexes could change on an evolutionary time scale (i.e. very slowly), for our purposes, the future will be pretty much the same as the present.

With some exceptions, however. Consider the case of pollutants called endocrine disruptors, or xenoestrogens, a large group of chemicals that mimic one or more hormones, blocking binding sites and disrupting normal endocrine function. These chemicals come from plastics, pesticides, and other products used in manufacturing and in daily life. In the past few years there has been great concern about plastic liners in water bottles because they contain a substance called Bisphenol A (BPA). The fear that exposure to BPA, especially from plastic baby bottles, could affect reproduction in future generations has been a boon for metal water bottle manufacturers. But questions about the actual danger of endocrine disruptors remain. Has the body burden of xenoestrogens caused a drop in sperm count, increased the frequency of

Everything develops

these bad thing affect our body

genital and gonadal malformations, impaired immune functions, caused cancers, and more?

There are no clear answers. But we do know that in the laboratory endocrine disruptors change cellular metabolism, and can cause tissue culture cells to grow abnormally. We also know that in the wild endocrine disruptor pollution from accidental chemical spills or from industrial byproducts has caused sex reversal or hermaphroditic gonad and genital development in frogs, fish, and alligators. Endocrine disruptors are everywhere; they are in our bodies already, but we could do more to reduce their presence around the world (Colburn, Dumanoski, & Meyers, 1997; Krimsky, 2002). For now we can say that they remain as a potential actor in the future of sex and gender.

Brains Can Change within a Single Generation

If the future of chromosomal, fetal hormonal, and genital sex seems pretty stable, brain sex may be less so. Brain anatomy changes with experiential input. Theoretically, then, changing physiological, physical, emotional, and cultural experiences could change brain sex. Some differences in men's and women's brain might lessen; new differences might appear. Consider the epithet hurled at a young boy that he "throws like a girl." Phenomenologist and neurologist Erwin Straus (1891–1975) described it this way: "The girl of five does not make any use of lateral space . . . All she does in preparation for throwing is to lift her right arm forward to the horizontal and to bend the forearm backward . . . The ball is released without force, speed or accurate aim . . . A boy of the same age . . . stretches his right arm sideward and backward; supinates the forearm; twists, turns and bends his trunk . . . The ball leaves the hand with considerable acceleration; it moves toward its goal in a long, flat curve" (cited in Young, 1990: 137).

By the time they are grown many American men have a smooth and forceful overhand throw. It "comes naturally." That is, they just do it without thinking through all the motions and positioning Straus described. They have developed connections between their central nervous system (the brain and spinal cord) and their motor system— not only the arm but the entire body—which positions itself as it executes a throw. If you scanned the brains of American men and women as they imagined throwing a ball, most likely you would find that for each sex different brain regions became activated. We associate the overhand throw with baseball, a national pastime, but not always an international one. So perhaps it is not surprising that anthropologist Greg Downey, who studies motorically skilled masters of the acrobatic dance form *capoeira*, in Brazil, noticed something quite interesting: most of his Brazilian male colleagues—talented athletes though they were—threw like girls (Downey, 2009).

As we learn motor activities our brains change. The first change that takes place during actual learning sessions is that nerve cell communication via synapses becomes more efficient. Continued practice leads to actual changes in the brain—specifically in that part of the cerebrum called the motor cortex (Rosenkranz, Kacar, & Rothwell, 2007). This is how we learn motor skills: our brain and motor system change anatomically in response to practice. So for girls and Brazilian men and other people who "throw like a girl" is this what's going on? It seems likely that even toddlers (in America) get training in how to throw. The training is hands on in many cases but also comes from observation. Watching baseball on TV or watching older siblings contribute to skill development. But for most boys it is probably just plain old play that does it. "The decisive ingredient seems to be the hundreds of idle hours spent throwing balls, sticks, rocks and so on in the playground or back yard" (Fallows, 1996).

Changes in Cultural Responses to Infant Gender Can Take Several Generations

Once a baby is visible (either at birth or via prenatal ultrasound) it becomes a social actor. Adults prepare its visual and tactile environment by buying toys, clothes, and room decorations. Especially during the first six months the primary caregiver and the infant form a single developmental unit and infant emotional systems develop within the dynamic of face-to-face interactions with the primary caregiver (Schore, 1994). This dynamical system relies especially on visual and auditory processing as the infant gazes at the mother's face. Information patterns in the mother's face trigger metabolic energy shifts in the infant. These changes in processes such as heart rate and respiration ultimately affect the growth and neural connectivity of specific brain regions. Schore believes these energy shifts form the basic features of embodied emotion (Schore, 2000).

In support of this idea, Wexler notes how basic parenting activities (holding and calming the baby, rocking the baby, speaking in repetitive tones) regulate and train infant physiology. Parental training of infant physiology includes calming, establishment of sleep cycles (Harkness, Super, Moscardino, Rha, Blom, Huitrón, et al., 2007), eating, and eliminative, as well as exploratory behaviors. As Wexler writes: "the influence of adults ... must shape neuronal circuitry in the developing brain of the infant and child" (Wexler, 2006: 103).

We have already seen that over a period of several decades the association of blue with girls and pink with boys switched. Today the world presented to an infant girl (especially in the United States—again this is not a universal phenomenon) is usually pretty pink, soft to the touch and filled with positive adult emotional feedback about girlish things. But as ideas about girlhood and boyhood change, and as adult gender roles change, it seems likely gendered, parent-driven aspects of parent–infant interactions will also alter. These may, in turn, shift gendered interests and certain skills in children and in the adults they become. Embedded cultural ideas change unevenly and take more than one generation. So while such change has happened in the past and will undoubtedly continue in the future, mapping their effects is likely to fall more to historians than to psychologists or anthropologists.

Changes in the Social and Legal Structures of Gender Can Happen in One Generation, or They Can Take Longer

Do sex and gender have a future, or, as some fear, will gender disappear (Kantrowitz & Wingert, 2010)? A quick Google of the phrase "gender free" brings up links to gender-free writing, raising a child gender free, gender-free contra dancing, and with a perverse switch of word order, free baby gender predictor. Clearly there is interest in eliminating gender distinctions from at least some parts of our culture, yet I doubt that we face a genderless future. Interest in sex and reproduction remains strong, and unless we achieve one of the feminist utopias in which reproduction becomes a neutral technology, partnering and having babies will continue to anchor some forms of sex and gender differentiation (Firestone, 1970; Piercy, 1985). But I do believe that individual gender variation will become better recognized and more acceptable. Gay marriage will become the law of the land, and many degrees of transgender will become socially unremarkable. The day may come when we don't have to designate "male" or "female" on our driver's licenses or passports, allowing people with gender presentations that don't match their natal sex the possibility of a freer existence. And, if much of this comes to pass, it is certain to feed back onto the development of gender in infants and children.

Of all of the points emphasized in this book, the one that needs most urgently to seep into people's ways of thought is that bodies are not bounded. To understand sex and gender we have to study how sensory, emotional, and motor experience becomes embodied. We will learn a lot about the science of sex and gender in the years to come. But to the extent that our social settings and thus experiences change, at least some of the subtleties of sex and gender will remain a moving target. This should keep life interesting and keep scientists employed if not out of trouble.

Further Reading

Patterson, Charlotte J. (2006). Children of lesbian and gay parents. *Current Directions in Psychological Science*, 15(5), 241–244.
Penn State. (2009). Male Sex Chromosome Losing Genes By Rapid Evolution, Study Reveals. *ScienceDaily* 17 July. Retrieved from: http://www.sciencedaily.com/releases/2009/07/090716201127.htm, accessed December 9, 2011.
The International Gender Bill of Rights (1995). Retrieved from: http://my.execpc.com/~dmmunson/billrights.htm, accessed December 9, 2011.

Thought Question

What laws exist that govern gender in America? Are any of them changing? (Hint: Google the phrase "Gender and the law" and follow some threads.) Can you think of any currently contested legal cases that might, over a few generations, change gender roles and even the biology of gender?

NOTES

2 Of Spirals and Layers

1. I clicked on "baby," then "baby clothes," then either "baby boy" (http://www.toysrus. com/search/index.jsp?categoryId=4021193&f=Taxonomy%2FTRUS%2F2255957& f=Taxonomy%2FTRUS%2F2255985&f=PAD%2FBoy+Girl%2FBoys&fbc=1&fbn= Boy+Girl%7CBoys&fbx=1), "baby girl" (http://www.toysrus.com/search/index.jsp?ca tegoryId=4021193&f=Taxonomy%2FTRUS%2F2255957&f=Taxonomy%2FTRUS %2F2255985&f=Taxonomy%2FTRUS%2F3243842&fbc=1&fbn=Taxonomy%7CBa by+Girl+Clothes&fbx=1), or "neutral" (http://www.toysrus.com/search/index.jsp?cate goryId=4021193&f=Taxonomy%2FTRUS%2F2255957&f=Taxonomy%2FTRUS%2 F2255985&f=Taxonomy%2FTRUS%2F3244773&fbc=1&fbn=Taxonomy%7CNeutr al&fbx=1). On the date of access (December 7, 2011) there were 265 baby boy items, 440 baby girl items, and 70 neutral items.

3 Of Molecules and Sex

1. Aphids, for example, have winged females that migrate to new plants and wingless females that reproduce without input from a male. Some of the winged females produce a male in the fall and the males mate with the females which then produce an egg that winters over. The eggs only hatch out wingless females in the spring (http:// en.wikipedia.org/wiki/Aphid#Reproduction).
2. Shoemaker and Crews write (2009: 300) "The pathway underlying mammalian testicular determination and differentiation has been elucidated more clearly and quickly than that underlying ovarian development..."
3. Temporary in mammals, but the cloaca remains into adulthood in many other vertebrates.
4. Social convention even affects scientific illustration. It is rarely noted that the embryonic phallus represented in Figure 3.3 is circumcised! Supposedly this representation makes it easier to see what the parts underneath the foreskin look like (or hood of the clitoris), but this can't be what the embryo itself really looks like.

4 Of Hormones and Brains

1. A *meme* is an idea, behavior, or style that spreads from person to person within a culture. While *genes* transmit biological information, memes are said to transmit ideas and belief information. A meme acts as a unit for carrying cultural ideas, symbols, or practices, which can be transmitted from one mind to another through writing, speech, gestures, rituals, or other imitable phenomena. Supporters of the concept regard memes as cultural analogues to genes in that they self-replicate, mutate, and respond to selective pressures. Retrieved from: http://en.wikipedia.org/wiki/Meme, accessed December 8, 2011.

2. This is the reason that parthenogenesis in mammals has a poor outcome. If there are two maternal chromosomes, then there are two copies of any imprinted genes, and thus no gene function for these loci. The result is fatal.

6 Thinking about Homosexuality

1. Portions of Chapter 6 are derived, with permission, from my book *Sexing the Body: Gender Politics and the Construction of Sexuality* (2000).

9 The Developmental Dynamics of Pink and Blue

1. Retrieved from: http://answers.yahoo.com/question/index?qid=20100604203056AAd Zkpt, accessed December 9, 2011.

REFERENCES

Aaronson, I. A., Cakmak, M. A., & Key, L. L. (1997). Defects of the testosterone biosynthetic pathway in boys with hypospadias. *Journal of Urology*, 157(May), 1884–1888.

Adams, R. J., & Courage, M. L. (1998). Human newborn color vision: measurement with chromatic stimuli varying in excitation purity. *Journal of Experimental Child Psychology*, 68(1), 22–34.

Alexander, G. M. (2003). An evolutionary perspective of sex-typed toy preferences: pink, blue, and the brain. *Archives of Sexual Behavior*, 32(1), 7–14.

Australian Institute of Health and Welfare, N.P.S.U. (2000). *Australia's Mothers and Babies* (p. 76). Canberra: Australian Institute of Health and Welfare.

Bagemihl, B. (1999). *Biological Exuberance: Animal Homosexuality and Natural Diversity*. New York: St. Martin's Press.

Bailey, J. M., Dunne, M. P., & Martin, N. G. (2000). Genetic and environmental influences on sexual orientation and its correlates in an Australian twin sample. *Journal of Personality and Social Psychology*, 78(3), 524–536.

Bailey, J. M., & Pillard, R. C. (1991a). Are some people born gay? *The New York Times*, December 17, p. A 21.

Bailey, J. M., & Pillard, R. C. (1991b). A genetic study of male sexual orientation. *Archives of General Psychiatry*, 48(12), 1089–1096.

Bailey, J. M., Willerman, L., & Parks, C. (1991). A test of the maternal stress theory of human male homosexuality. *Archives of Sexual Behavior*, 20(3), 277–293.

Bandura, A., & Bussey, K. (2004). On broadening the cognitive, motivational, and socio-structural scope of theorizing about gender development and functioning: comment on Martin, Ruble, and Szkrybalo (2002). *Psychological Bulletin*, 130(5), 691–701.

Bell, G. (2008). *Sex and Death in Protozoa: The History of Obsession*. Cambridge: Cambridge University Press.

Bem, D. J. (2008). Is there a causal link between childhood gender nonconformity and adult homosexuality? *Journal of Gay and Lesbian Mental Health*, 12(1/2), 61–80.

Berenbaum, S. A., & Snyder, E. (1995). Early hormonal influences on childhood sex-typed activity and playmate preferences: implications for the development of sexual orientation. *Developmental Psychology*, 31(1), 31–42.

Berkman, A. (1912). *Prison Memoirs of an Anarchist*. New York: Mother Earth Publishing Association.

Blackless, M., Charuvastra, A., Derryck, A., Fausto-Sterling, A., Lauzanne, K., & Lee, E. (2000). How sexually dimorphic are we? A review article. *American Journal of Human Biology*, 12(2), 151–166.

Bocklandt, S., & Vilain, E. (2007). Sex differences in brain and behavior: hormones versus genes. *Advances in Genetics*, 59, 245–266.

Bolt Blitz in Oslo; Athletics (2011). *The Age*, June 11, p. 25. Melbourne.

Boman, U. W., Möller, A., & Albertsson-Wikland, K. (1998). Psychological aspects of Turner Syndrome. *Journal of Psychosomatic Obstetrics and Gynaecology*, 19(1), 1–18.

Bornstein, K. (1994). *Gender Outlaw: On Men, Women and the Rest of Us*. London: Routledge.

Boswell, J. (1990). Sexual and ethical categories in premodern Europe. In D. P. McWhirter, S. A. Sanders, & J. M. Reinisch (Eds.), *Homosexuality/Heterosexuality: Concepts of Sexual Orientation* (pp. 15–31). New York, NY: Oxford University Press.

Bromberg-Martin, E. S., Matsumoto, M., & Hikosaka, O. (2010). Dopamine in motivational control: rewarding, aversive, and alerting. *Neuron*, 68(5), 815–834.

Bromley, B., Frigoletto, F. D., Jr., Harlow, B. L., Evans, J. K., & Benacerraf, B. R. (1993). Biometric measurements in fetuses of different race and gender. *Ultrasound in Obstetrics and Gynecology*, 3, 395–402.

Byne, W. (1997). Why we cannot conclude that sexual orientation is primarily a biological phenomenon. *Journal of Homosexuality*, 34(1), 73–80.

Byne, W., Lasco, M. S., Kemether, E., Shinwari, A., Edgar, M. A., Morgello, S., et al. (2000). The interstitial nuclei of the human anterior hypothalamus: an investigation of sexual variation in volume and cell size, number and density. *Brain Research*, 856(1–2), 254–258.

Byne, W., Tobet, S., Mattiace, L. A., Lasco, M. S., Kemether, E., Edgar, M. A., et al. (2001). The interstitial nuclei of the human anterior hypothalamus: an investigation of variation with sex, sexual orientation and HIV status. *Hormones and Behavior*, 40(2), 86–92.

Caster Semenya (2010). Retrieved from: http://www.wikipedia.org, accessed December 10, 2011.

Center for Disease Control (2000). 2000 CDC growth charts: United States. Retrieved from: http://www.cdc.gov/growthcharts, accessed December 13, 2011.

Chiu, S. W., Gervan, S., Fairbrother, C., Johnson, L. L., Owen-Anderson, A. F. H., Bradley, S., et al. (2006). Sex-dimorphic color preference in children with Gender Identity Disorder: a comparison to clinical and community controls. *Sex Roles*, 55, 385–395.

Colapinto, J. (2001). *As Nature Made Him: The Boy Who Was Raised as a Girl*. New York: Harper.

Colburn, T., Dumanoski, D., & Meyers, J. P. (1997). *Our Stolen Future: Are We Threatening Our Fertility, Intelligence, and Survival?—A Scientific Detective Story*. New York: Plume.

Conte, F. A., & Grumbach, M. A. (1989). Pathogenesis, classification, diagnosis, and treatment of anomalies of sex. In L. De Groot (Ed.), *Endocrinology* (pp. 1810–1847). Philadelphia, PA: Saunders.

Cook, C.D.K. (1968) Phenotypic plasticity with particular reference to three amphibious plant species. In V. Heywood (Ed.), *Modern Methods in Plant Taxonomy* (pp. 97–111). London: Academic Press.

Corbett, K. (1993). The mystery of homosexuality. *Psychoanalytic Psychology*, 10(3), 345–357.

Corbett, K. (1996). Homosexual boyhood: notes on girlyboys. *Gender and Psychoanalysis*, 1, 429–461.

Cramer, J. S., & Lumey, L. H. (2010). Maternal preconception diet and the sex ratio. *Human Biology*, 82(1), 103–107.

Crawford, M., Doyle, W., & Meadows, N. (1987). Gender differences at birth and differences in fetal growth. *Human Reproduction*, 2(6), 517–520.

Crews, D., & Fitzgerald, K. T. (1980). "Sexual" behavior in parthenogenetic lizards. *Proceedings of the National Academy of Sciences US*, 77(1), 499–502.

Crognale, M. A., Kelly, J. P., Weiss, A. H., & Teller, D. Y. (1998). Development of the spatio-chromatic visual evoked potential (VEP): a longitudinal study. *Vision Research*, 38(21), 3283–3292.

Davis, D. L., & Whitten, R. G. (1987). The cross-cultural study of human sexuality. *Annual Review of Anthropology*, 16, 69–98.

Davis, R., Cutter, G., Goldenberg, R., Hoffman, H., Cliver, S., & Brumfield, C. (1993). Fetal biparietal diameter, head circumference, abdominal circumference and femur length. A comparison by race and sex. *Journal of Reproductive Medicine*, 38(3), 201–206.

Diamond, L. M. (2007). A dynamical systems approach to the development and expression of female same-sex sexuality. *Perspectives in Psychological Science*, 2(2), 142–161.

Diamond, L. M. (2008). *Sexual Fluidity: Understanding Women's Love and Desire*. Cambridge, MA: Harvard University Press.

Diamond, M. (1965). A critical evaluation of the ontogeny of human sexual behavior. *Quarterly Review of Biology*, 40, 147–175.

Diamond, M., & Sigmundson, K. (1997). Sex reassignment at birth: long-term review and clinical implications. *Archives of Pediatric and Adolescent Medicine*, 151(March), 298–304.

DiNapoli, L., & Capel, B. (2008). SRY and the standoff in sex determination. *Molecular Endocrinology*, 22(1), 1–9.

Dittman, R. W., Kappes, M. H., Kappes, M. E., Börger, D., Willig, R. H., & Wallis, H. (1990). Congenital adrenal hyperplasia I: gender-related behavior and attitudes in female patients and sisters. *Psychoneuroendocrinology*, 15(5 & 6), 401–420.

Dobkins, K. R., Bosworth, R. G., & McCleery, J. P. (2009). Effects of gestational length, gender, postnatal age, and birth order on visual contrast sensitivity in infants. *Journal of Vision*, 9(10), 19, 1–21.

Dörner, G., Schenk, B., Schmiedel, B., & Ahrens, L. (1983). Stressful events in prenatal life of bi- and homosexual men. *Experimental and Clinical Endocrinology*, 81(1), 83–87.

Downey, G. (2009, February 1). Throwing like a girl's brain. Retrieved from: http://neuroan-thropology.net/2009/02/01/throwing-like-a-girls-brain, accessed December 10, 2011.

Dreger, A. D. (1998a). "Ambiguous sex"—or ambivalent medicine? Ethical issues in the treatment of intersexuality. *Hastings Center Report* (May–June), 24–35.

Dreger, A. D. (1998b). *Hermaphrodites and the Medical Invention of Sex*. Cambridge, MA: Harvard University Press.

Duden, B. (1991). *The Woman Beneath the Skin*. Cambridge, MA: Harvard University Press.

Eichstedt, J. A., Serbin, L. A., Poulin-Dubois, D., & Sen, M. G. (2002). Of bears and men: infants' knowledge of conventional and metaphorical gender stereotypes. *Infant Behavior and Development*, 25(3), 296–310.

Ellis, H. (1913). *Studies in the Psychology of Sex*. Philadelphia, PA: F.A. Davis.

Epstein, Brad M. (2009). *New York Yankees ABC My First Alphabet Book*. Aliso Viejo, CA:. Michaelson Entertainment.

Fagot, B. I., & Leinbach, M. D. (1989). The young child's gender schema: environmental input, internal organization. *Child Development*, 60, 663–672.

Fagot, B. I., & Leinbach, M. D. (1993). Gender-role development in young children: from discrimination to labeling. *Developmental Review*, 13, 205–224.

Fagot, B. I., Leinbach, M. D., & Hagan, R. (1986). Gender labeling and the adoption of sex-typed behaviors. *Developmental Psychology*, 22(4), 440–443.

Fagot, B. I., Leinbach, M. D., & O'Boyle, C. (1992). Gender labeling, gender stereotyping, and parenting behaviors. *Developmental Psychology*, 28(2), 225–230.

Fallows, J. (1996). Throwing like a girl. *The Atlantic Monthly*. Retrieved from: http://www.theatlantic.com/past/docs/issues/96aug/throw/throw.htm, accessed December 12, 2011.

Fausto-Sterling, A. (1989). Life in the XY corral. *Women's Studies International Forum*, 12(3), 319–331.

Fausto-Sterling, A. (2000). *Sexing the Body: Gender Politics and the Construction of Sexuality*. New York: Basic Books.

Fausto-Sterling, A. (2012). The dynamic development of gender variability. *Journal of Homosexuality*, in press.

Fausto-Sterling, A., García Coll, C., & Lamarre, M. (2011a). Sexing the baby: Part 1 What do we really know about sex differentiation in the first year of life? *Social Science and Medicine*, doi:10.1016/j.socscimed.2011.05.051.

Fausto-Sterling, A., García Coll, C., & Lamarre, M. (2011b). Sexing the baby: Part 2 Applying Dynamic Systems Theory to the emergences of sex-related differences in infants and toddlers. *Social Science and Medicine*, doi:10.1016/j.socscimed.2011.06.027.

Feinberg, L. (1996). *Transgender Warriors*. Boston: Beacon Press.

Feinberg, L. (1998). *Trans Liberation: Beyond Pink or Blue*. Boston: Beacon Press.

Fine, C. (2010). *Delusions of Gender*. New York: W.W. Norton and Company.

Firestone, S. (1970). *The Dialectic of Sex: The Case for Feminist Revolution*. New York: Farrar, Straus and Giroux.

Foucault, M. (1978). *The History of Sexuality*. New York: Pantheon.

Franklin, A., Bevis, L., Ling, Y., & Hurlbert, A. (2010). Biological components of colour preference in infancy. *Developmental Science*, 13(2), 346–354.

Franklin, A., & Davies, I. R. L. (2004). New evidence for infant colour categories. *British Journal of Developmental Psychology*, 22, 349 n.377.

Frassanito, P., & Pettorini, B. (2008). Pink and blue: the color of gender. *Child's Nervous System*, 24(8), 881–882.

Gahr, M., Metzdorf, R., Schmidl, D., & Wickler, W. (2008). Bi-directional sexual dimorphisms of the song control nucleus HVC in a songbird with unison song. *Public Library of Science One*, 3(8), e3073.

Gahr, M., Sonnenschein, E., & Wickler, W. (1998). Sex difference in the size of the neural song control regions in a dueting songbird with similar song repertoire size of males and females. *Journal of Neuroscience*, 18(3), 1124–1131.

Gastaud, F., Bouvattier, C., Duranteau, L., Brauner, R., Thibaud, E., Kutten, F., et al. (2007). Impaired sexual and reproductive outcomes in women with classical forms of congenital adrenal hyperplasia. *Journal of Clinical Endocrinology Metabolism*, 92(4), 1391–1396.

Giedd, J. N., Castellanos, F. X., Rajapakse, J. C., Vaituzis, A. C., & Rapoport, J. L. (1997). Sexual dimorphism of the developing human brain. *Progress in Neuropsychopharmacology and Biological Psychiatry*, 21(8), 1185–1201.

Gilbert, S. (2010). *Developmental Biology*. Sunderland, MA: Sinauer Associates.

Gladue, B. A., Beatty, W. W., Larson, J., & Staton, R. D. (1990). Sexual orientation and spatial ability in men and women. *Psychobiology*, 18(1), 101–108.

Godwin, J. (2010). Neuroendocrinology of sexual plasticity in teleost fishes. *Frontiers in Neuroendocrinology*, 31(2), 203–216.

Goldberg, A. B. (2007). Born with the wrong body: transgender 10-year-old girl and her family talk to Barbara Walters. ABC News: 20/20. USA. April 25.

Green, R. (2008). Childhood cross-gender behavior and adult homosexuality: why the link? *Journal of Gay and Lesbian Mental Health*, 12(1/2), 17–28.

Green, R. (2010). Robert Stoller's sex and gender: 40 years on. *Archives of Sexual Behavior*, 39(6), 1457–1465.

Gregg, C., Zhang, J., Butler, J. E., Haig, D., & Dulac, C. (2010). Sex-specific parent-of-origin allelic expression in the mouse brain. *Science*, 329(5992), 682–685.

Gregg, C., Zhang, J., Weissbourd, B., Luo, S., Schroth, G. P., Haig, D., et al. (2010). High-resolution analysis of parent-of-origin allelic expression in the mouse brain. *Science*, 329(5992), 643–648.

Gross, M. R., & Charnov, E. L. (1980). Alternative male life histories in bluegill sunfish. *Proceedings of the National Academy of Sciences, US*, 77(11), 6937–6940.

Hall, J. A. Y., & Kimura, D. (1995). Sexual orientation and perfomrance on sexually dimorphic motor tasks. *Archives of Sexual Behavior*, 24(4), 395–407.

Hamer, D., Hu, S., Magnuson, V. L., Hu, N., & Pattatucci, A. M. L. (1993). Linkage between DNA markers on the X chromosome and male sexual orientation. *Science*, 261, 321–325.

Hansen, B. (1989). American physicians' earliest writings about homosexuals, 1880–1900. *The Milbank Quarterly*, 67(Supplement 1), 92–108.

Hansen, B. (1992). American physicians' "discovery" of homosexuals, 1880–1900: a new diagnosis in a changing society. In C. Rosenberg & J. Golden (Eds.), *Framing Disease* (pp. 104–133). New Brunswick, NJ: Rutgers University Press.

Harkness, S., Super, C. M., Moscardino, U., Rha, J.-H., Blom, M., Huitrón, B., et al. (2007). Cultural models and developmental agendas: implications for arousal and self-regulation in early infancy. *Journal of Developmental Processes*, 2(1), 5–39.

Harley, V. R., Clarkson, M. J., & Argentaro, A. (2003). The molecular action and regulation of the testis-determining factors, SRY (sex-determining region on the Y chromosome) and SOX9 [SRY-related high-mobility group (HMG) box 9]. *Endocrine Reviews*, 24(4), 466–487.

Hayles, N. K. (1993). The materiality of informatics. *Configurations*, 1(1), 147–170.

Hendricks, S. E., Graber, B., & Rodriguez-Sierra, J. F. (1989). Neuroendocrine responses to exogenous estrogen: no differences between heterosexual and homosexual men. *Psychoneuroendocrinology*, 14(3), 177–185.

Herdt, G. (1990). Developmental discontinuities and sexual orientation across cultures. In D. P. McWhirter, S. Sanders, A. & J. M. Reinisch (Eds.), *Homosexuality/Heterosexuality*. New York: Oxford University Press.

Hill, D. B., Menvielle, E., Sica, K. M., & Johnson, A. (2010). An affirmative intervention for families with gender variant children: parental ratings of child mental health and gender. *Journal of Sex and Marital Therapy*, 36(1), 6–23.

Hines, M. (2009). Gonadal hormones and sexual differentiation of human brain and behavior. In D. W. Pfaff, A. P. Arnold, A. M. Etgen, S. E. Fahrbach, & R. T. Rubin (Eds.), *Hormones, Brain and Behavior*, 2nd ed. (pp. 1869–1909). San Diego, CA: Academic Press.

Hines, M., Brook, C., & Conway, G. S. (2004). Androgen and psychosexual development: core gender identity, sexual orientation and recalled childhood gender role behavior in women and men with congenital adrenal hyperplasia (CAH). *Journal of Sex Research*, 41(1), 75–81.

Hines, M., Golombok, S., Rust, J., Johnston, K. J., & Golding, J. (2002). Testosterone during pregnancy and gender role behavior of preschool children: a longitudinal, population study. *Child Development*, 73(6), 1678–1687.

Hines, M., Johnston, K. J., Golombok, S., Rust, J., Stevens, M., & Golding, J. (2002). Prenatal stress and gender role behavior in girls and boys: a longitudinal, population study. *Hormones and Behavior*, 42(2), 126–134.

Hines, M., & Kaufman, F. R. (1994). Androgen and the development of human sex-typical behavior: rough-and-tumble play and sex of preferred playmates in children with congenital adrenal hyperplasia (CAH). *Child Development*, 65(4), 1042–1053.

Hyde, J. S. (2005). The gender similarities hypothesis. *American Psychologist*, 60(6), 581–592.

Hyde, J. S. (2007). New directions in the study of gender similarities and differences. *Current Directions in Psychological Science*, 16, 259–263.

Hyde, J. S., Lindberg, S. M., Linn, M. C., Ellis, A. B., & Williams, C. C. (2008). Diversity. Gender similarities characterize math performance. *Science*, 321(5888), 494–495.

Jacobs, P., Dalton, P., James, R., Mosse, K., Power, M., Robinson, D., et al. (1997). Turner Syndrome: a cytogenetic and molecular study. *Annals of Human Genetics*, 61, 471–483.

Jadva, V., Hines, M., & Golombok, S. (2010). Infants' preferences for toys, colors, and shapes: sex differences and similarities. *Archives of Sexual Behavior*, 39(6), 1261–1273.

Jordan-Young, R. M. (2010). *Brain Storm: The Flaws in the Science of Sex Differences*. Cambridge, MA: Harvard University Press.

Juraska, J. M. (1991). Sex differences in "cognitive" regions of the rat brain. *Psychoneuroendocrinology*, 16(1–3), 105–109.

Kantrowitz, B., & Wingert, P. (2010). Are we facing a genderless future? *Newsweek*, August 16. Retrieved from: http://www.thedailybeast.com/newsweek/2010/08/16/life-without-gender.print.html, acccessed December 11, 2011.

Katz, J. N. (1995). *The Invention of Heterosexuality*. New York: Dutton.

Kegel, C. A. T., Bus, A. G., & van Ijzendoorn, M. H. (2011). Differential susceptibility in early literacy instruction through computer games: the role of the Dopamine D4 Receptor gene (DRD4). *Mind, Brain and Education*, 5(2), 71–78.

Keller, E. F. (2010). *The Mirage of a Space between Nature and Nurture*. Durham, NC: Duke University Press.

Kessler, S. (1998). *Lessons from the Intersexed*. New Brunswick, NJ: Rutgers University Press.

Kessler, S. J., & McKenna, W. (1978). *Gender: An Ethnomethodological Approach*. New York: John Wiley & Sons.

Kiely, M. M., Xu, F., McGeehin, M., Jackson, R., & Sinks, T. (1999). Changing sex ratio in the United States, 1969–1995. *Fertility and Sterility*, 71(5), 969–971.

Kinsey, A. C., Pomeroy, W. B., & Martin, C. E. (1948). *Sexual Behavior in the Human Male*. Philadelphia, PA: W.B. Saunders Co.

Kinsey, A. C., Pomeroy, W. B., Martin, C. E., & Gebhard, P. H. (1953). *Sexual Behavior in the Human Female*. Philadelphia, PA: W.B. Saunders Co.

Krafft-Ebing, R. v. (1892). *Psychopathia Sexualis, with Especial Reference to Contrary Sexual Instinct: A Medico-Legal Study*. Philadelphia, PA: F.A. Davis.

Kramer, M. S. (1987). Determinants of low birth weight: methodological assessment and meta-analysis. *Bulletin of the World Health Organization*, 65(5), 663–737.

Krimsky, S. (2002). *Hormonal Chaos: The Scientific and Social Origins of the Environmental Endocrine Hypothesis*. Baltimore, MD: Johns Hopkins University Press.

Kruijver, F. P., Zhou, J. N., Pool, C. W., Hofman, M. A., Gooren, L. J., & Swaab, D. F. (2000). Male-to-female transsexuals have female neuron numbers in a limbic nucleus. *Journal of Clinical Endocrinology & Metabolism*, 85(5), 2034–2041.

Langer, S. J., & Martin, J. I. (2004). How dresses can make you mentally ill: examining Gender Identity Disorder in children. *Child and Adolescent Social Work Journal*, 21, 5–23.

Laumann, E. O., Gagnon, J. H., Michael, R. T., & Michaels, S. (1994). *The Social Organization of Sexuality: Sexual Practices in the United States*. Chicago: University of Chicago Press.

Lawrence, A. (2007). A critique of the brain-sex theory of transsexualism. Retrieved from: http://www.annelawrence.com/twr/brain-sex_critique.html, accessed December 10, 2011.

Lawrence, A. (2008). Gender Identity Disorders in adults: diagnosis and treatment. In D. L. Rowland & L. Incrocci (Eds.), *Handbook of Sexual and Gender Identity* (pp. 423–456). New York: John Wiley and Sons.

LeVay, S. (1991). A difference in hypothalamic structure between heterosexual and homosexual men. *Science*, 253, 1034–1037.

Levy, G. D., & Haaf, R. A. (1994). Detection of gender-related categories by 10-month-old infants. *Infant Behavior & Development*, 17, 457–459.

Lippa, R. A. (2006). The Gender Reality Hypothesis. *American Psychologist*, 61(6), 639.

Lorber, J. (1994). *Paradoxes of Gender*. New Haven, CT: Yale University Press.

Martin, C. L., Ruble, D. N., & Szkrybalo, J. (2002). Cognitive theories of early gender development. *Psychological Bulletin*, 128(6), 903–933.

Martin, C. L., Ruble, D. N., & Szkrybalo, J. (2004). Recognizing the centrality of gender identity and stereotype knowledge in gender development and moving toward theoretical integration: reply to Bandura and Bussey. *Psychological Bulletin*, 130(5), 702–710.

Martin, J. I. (2008). Nosology, etiology, and course of Gender Identity Disorder. *Journal of Gay and Lesbian Mental Health*, 12(1/2), 81–94.

McCarthy, M. M., & Konkle, A. T. (2005). When is a sex difference not a sex difference? *Frontiers in Neuroendocrinology*, 26(2), 85–102.

McCormick, C. M., & Witelson, S. F. (1991). A cognitive profile of homosexual men compared to heterosexual men and women. *Psychoneuroendocrinology*, 16(6), 459–473.

McIntosh, M. (1968). The homosexual role. *Social Problems*, 16, 182–192.

Menvielle, E., & Hill, D. B. (2011). An affirmative intervention for families with gender-variant children: a process evaluation. *Journal of Gay and Lesbian Mental Health*, 15, 94–123.

Menvielle, E., & Tuerk, C. (2002). A support group for parents of gender-nonconforming boys. *Journal of the American Academy of Child and Adolescent Psychiatry*, 41(8), 1010–1013.

Menvielle, E. J., Tuerk, C., & Perrin, E. C. (2005, February 1). To the beat of a different drummer: the gender variant child. Retrieved from: http://www.imatyfa.org/permanent_files/to-the-beat-of-a-different-drummer-6-2007.pdf, accessed December 11, 2011.

Meyer-Bahlburg, H. F. (2005). Gender identity outcome in female-raised 46, XY persons with penile agenesis, cloacal exstrophy of the bladder, or penile ablation. *Archives of Sexual Behavior*, 34(4), 423–438.

Meyer-Bahlburg, H., Ehrhardt, A. A., Rosen, L. R., Gruen, R. S., Veridiano, N. P., Vann, F. H., et al. (1995). Prenatal estrogens and the development of homosexual orientation. *Developmental Psychology*, 31(1), 12–21

Meyerowitz, J. (2002). *How Sex Changed: A History of Transsexuality in the United States*. Cambridge, MA: Harvard University Press.

Money, J., & Ehrhardt, A. A. (1972). *Man and Woman, Boy and Girl*. Baltimore, MD: Johns Hopkins University Press.

Morris, J. A., Jordan, C. L., & Breedlove, S. M. (2004). Sexual differentiation of the vertebrate nervous system. *Nature Neuroscience*, 7(10), 1034–1039.

Mustanski, B. S., Chivers, M. L., & Bailey, J. M. (2002). A critical review of recent biological research on human sexual orientation. *Annual Review of Sex Research*, 13, 89–140.

Neitz, J., Carroll, J., Yamauchi, Y., Neitz, M., & Williams, D. R. (2002). Color perception is mediated by a plastic neural mechanism that is adjustable in adults. *Neuron*, 35(4), 783–792.

Ngun, T. C., Ghahramani, N., Sanchez, F. J., Bocklandt, S., & Vilain, E. (2010). The genetics of sex differences in brain and behavior. *Frontiers in Neuroendocrinology*, 2(2), 227–246.

Nottebohm, F., & Arnold, A. P. (1976). Sexual dimorphism in vocal control areas of the songbird brain. *Science*, 194(4261), 211–213.

Nye, R. A. (1998). Introduction. In R. A. Nye (Ed.), *Oxford Readers: Sexuality* (pp. 3–15). Oxford: Oxford University Press.

Ortner, S. B. (1996). *Making Gender: The Politics and Erotics of Culture*. Boston: Beacon Press.

Oyewumi, O. (1998). De-confounding gender: feminist theorizing and western culture, a comment on Hawkesworth's "Confounding gender." *Signs*, 23(4), 1049–1062.

Paoletti, J. B. (1987). Clothing and gender in America: children's fashions 1890–1920. *Signs*, 13(1), 136–143.

Paoletti, J. B. (1997). The gendering of infants' and toddlers' clothing in America. In K. Martinez & K. L. Amers (Eds.), *The Material Culture of Gender; The Gender of Material Culture* (pp. 27–35). Hanover, NH: University Press of New England.

Parma, P., Radi, O., Vidal, V., Chaboissier, M. C., Dellambra, E., Valentini, S., et al. (2006). R-spondin1 is essential in sex determination, skin differentiation and malignancy. *Nature Genetics*, 38(11), 1304–1309.

Piercy, M. (1985). *Woman on the Edge of Time*. New York: Fawcett.

Poulin-Dubois, D., Serbin, L. A., & Derbyshire, A. (1998). Toddlers' intermodal and verbal knowledge about gender. *Merrill Palmer Quarterly*, 44(3), 338–354.

Poulin-Dubois, D., Serbin, L. A., Eichstedt, J. A., Sen, M. G., & Beissel, C. F. (2002). Men don't put on make-up: toddlers' knowledge of the gender stereotyping of household activities. *Social Development*, 11(2), 166–181.

Poulin-Dubois, D., Serbin, L. A., Kenyon, B., & Derbyshire, A. (1994). Infants' intermodal knowledge about gender. *Developmental Psychology*, 30(3), 436–442.

Quinn, P. C., Yahr, J., Kuhn, A., Slater, A. M., & Pascalils, O. (2002). Representation of the gender of human faces by infants: a preference for female. *Perception*, 31(9), 1109–1121.

Rametti, G., Carrillo, B., Gómez-Gil, E., Junque, C., Segovia, S., Gomez, Á., et al. (2011a). White matter microstructure in female to male transsexuals before cross-sex hormonal treatment. A diffusion tensor imaging study. *Journal of Psychiatric Research*, 45(2), 199–204.

Rametti, G., Carrillo, B., Gómez-Gil, E., Junque, C., Zubiarre-Elorza, L., Segovia, S., et al. (2011b). The microstructure of white matter in male to female transsexuals before cross-sex hormonal treatment. A DTI study. *Journal of Psychiatric Research*, 45(7), 949–954.

Rivers, J., & Crawford, M. (1974). Maternal nutrition and the sex ratio at birth. *Nature*, 252, 297–298.

Rosenfeld, C. S., & Roberts, R. M. (2004). Maternal diet and other factors affecting offspring sex ratio: a review. *Biology of Reproduction*, 71(4), 1063–1070.

Rosenkranz, K., Kacar, A., & Rothwell, J. C. (2007). Differential modulation of motor cortical plasticity and excitability in early and late phases of human motor learning. *Journal of Neuroscience*, 27(44), 12058–12066.

Rosenstein, L. D., & Bigler, E. D. (1987). No relationship between handedness and sexual preference. *Psychological Reports*, 60(3 Pt 1), 704–706.

Ruble, D., & Martin, C. L. (1998). Gender development. In N. Eisenberg (Ed.), *Social, Emotional and Personality Development* (pp. 933–1016). New York: Wiley.

Ruble, D. N., Martin, C. L., & Berenbaum, S. A. (Eds.) (2006). *Gender Development*. Hoboken, NJ: John Wiley and Sons.

Rust, J., Golombok, S., Hines, M., Johnston, K., & Golding, J. (2000). The role of brothers and sisters in the gender development of preschool children. *Journal of Experimental Child Psychology*, 77(4), 292–303.

Sandfort, T. G. M. (2005). Sexual orientation and gender: stereotypes and beyond. *Archives of Sexual Behavior*, 34(6), 595–611.

Schore, A. N. (1994). *Affect Regulation and the Origin of the Self: The Neurobiology of Emotional Development*. Hillsdale, NJ: L. Erlbaum Associates.

Schore, A. N. (2000). The self organization of the right brain and the neurobiology of emotional development. In M. D. Lewis & I. Granic (Eds.), *Emotional Development and Self Organization: Dynamic Systems Approach to Emotional Development.* Cambridge: Cambridge University Press.

Seager, J. (2003). *The Penguin Atlas of Women in the World.* London: Myriad Editions.

Serbin, L. A., Poulin-Dubois, D., Colburne, K. A., Sen, M. G., & Eichstedt, J. A. (2001). Gender stereotyping in infancy: visual preferences for and knowledge of gender-stereotyped toys in the second year. *International Journal of Behavioral Development,* 25(1), 7–15.

Serbin, L. A., Poulin-Dubois, D., & Eichstedt, J. A. (2002). Infants' response to gender-inconsistent events. *Infancy,* 3(4), 531–542.

Shoemaker, C. M., & Crews, D. (2009). Analyzing the coordinated gene network underlying temperature-dependent sex determination in reptiles. *Seminars in Cell and Developmental Biology,* 20(3), 293–303.

Simerly, R. B. (2002). Wired for reproduction: organization and development of sexually dimorphic circuits in the mammalian forebrain. *Annual Review of Neuroscience,* 25, 507–536.

Spiegel, A. (2008a). Parents consider treatment to delay son's puberty: new therapy would buy time to resolve gender crisis. *All Things Considered,* May 7. National Public Radio, USA.

Spiegel, A. (2008b). Two families grapple with sons' gender preferences: psychologists take radically different approaches in therapy. *All Things Considered,* May 8. National Public Radio, USA.

Steensma, T. D., Biemond, R., Boer, F. D., & Cohen-Kettenis, P. T. (2011). Desisting and persisting gender dysphoria after childhood: a qualitative follow-up study. *Clinical Child Psychology and Psychiatry,* 16(4), 499–516.

Stein, E. (1998). Review of Queer Science: the use and abuse of research on homosexuality. *Journal of Homosexuality,* 35(2), 107–117.

Stiles, J. (2008). *The Fundamentals of Brain Development: Integrating Nature and Nurture.* Cambridge, MA: Harvard University Press.

Strock, C. (1998). *Married Women Who Love Women.* New York: Doubleday.

Stryker, S., & Whittle, S. (Eds.) (2006). *The Transgender Studies Reader.* New York: Routledge.

Sugita, Y. (2004). Experience in early infancy is indispensable for color perception. *Current Biology,* 14(14), 1267–1271.

Teller, D. Y. (1998). Spatial and temporal aspects of infant color vision. *Vision Research,* 38(21), 3275–3282.

Thelen, E. (1995). Motor development: a new synthesis. *American Psychologist,* 50(2), 79–95.

Thelen, E. (2000). Grounded in the world: developmental origins of the embodied mind. *Infancy,* 1(1), 3–28.

Thelen, E., & Smith, L. B. (1994). *A Dynamic Systems Approach to the Development of Cognition and Action.* Cambridge, MA: MIT Press.

Tomizuka, K., Horikoshi, K., Kitada, R., Sugawara, Y., Iba, Y., Kojima, A., et al. (2008). R-spondin1 plays an essential role in ovarian development through positively regulating Wnt-4 signaling. *Human Molecular Genetics,* 17(9), 1278–1291.

van Vliet, G., Liu, S., & Kramer, M. (2009). Decreasing sex difference in birth weight. *Epidemiology,* 20(4), 622.

Vance, C. S. (1991). Anthropology rediscovers sexuality: a theoretical comment. *Social Science and Medicine,* 33(8), 875–884.

Veitia, R. A. (2010). FOXL2 versus SOX9: a lifelong "battle of the sexes." *Bioessays,* 32(5), 375–380.

Wade, N. (2010). Tug of war pits genes of parents in the fetus. *New York Times*, September 13, p. 5. New York.

Weinraub, M., Clemens, L. P., Sockloff, A., Ethridge, T., Gracely, E., & Myers, B. (1984). The development of sex role stereotypes in the third year: relationships to gender labeling, gender identity, sex-typed toy preference, and family characteristics. *Child Development*, 55(4), 1493–1503.

Weinrich, J. D. (1987). *Sexual Landscapes: Why We Are What We Are; Why We Love Whom We Love*. New York: Charles Scribner's Sons.

Weston, K. (1993). Lesbian and gay studies in the house of anthropology. *Annual Review of Anthropology*, 22, 339–367.

Wexler, B. E. (2006). *Brain and Culture: Neurobiology, Ideology and Social Change*. Cambridge, MA: MIT Press.

Wilhelm, D., Palmer, S., & Koopman, P. (2007). Sex determination and gonadal development in mammals. *Physiological Reviews*, 87(1), 1–28.

Winfrey, O. (August 24, 2004). The 11-year-old who wants a sex change. *The Oprah Winfrey Show*. USA.

Yoon, J. (2006). The Pink and Blue Project. Retrieved from: http://www.jeongmeeyoon.com/aw_pinkblue.htm, accessed February 2012.

Young, I. M. (1990). *Throwing Like a Girl and Other Essays in Feminist Philosophy and Social Theory*. Bloomington: Indiana University Press.

Zhou, J. N., Hofman, M. A., Gooren, L. J., & Swaab, D. F. (1995). A sex difference in the human brain and its relation to transsexuality. *Nature*, 378(6552), 68–70.

Zucker, K. J. (2008). Reflections of the relation between sex-typed behavior in childhood and sexual orientation in adulthood. *Journal of Gay and Lesbian Mental Health*, 12(1/2), 29–59.

Zucker, K. J., & Cohen-Kettenis, P. T. (2008). Gender Identity Disorder in children and adolescents. In D. L. Rowland & L. Incrocci (Eds.), *Handbook of Sexual and Gender Identity Disorders* (pp. 376–422). New York: John Wiley and Sons.

ACKNOWLEDGMENTS

Figures 2.1, 4.3, 6.1, 6.2, Tables 2.1, 3.1 From Anne Fausto-Sterling, *Sexing the Body: Gender Politics and the Construction of Sexuality.* Copyright © 2000 by Anne Fausto-Sterling. Reprinted with the permission of Basic Books, Inc., a member of Perseus Books Group.

Figure 2.2 Adapted from J. Money and A. A. Ehrhardt, *Man and Woman, Boy and Girl* (Baltimore: The Johns Hopkins University Press, 1972), p. 3. Copyright © 1972. Adapted with permission.

Figure 2.3 From JeongMee Yoon, "The Pink and Blue Project" (2006). Reprinted with permission of the artist.

Figure 3.1 Adapted from C. M. Shoemaker and D. Crews, "Analyzing the coordinated gene network underlying temperature-dependent sex determination in reptiles" from *Seminars in Cell and Developmental Biology*, 20(3): 296, Figure 1. Reprinted with the permission of Elsevier Science Limited.

Figure 3.2 From S. Gilbert, *Developmental Biology*, Figure 3.2. Copyright © 2010. Reprinted with the permission of Sinauer Associates, Inc., Publishers.

Figure 3.3 From Keith L. Moore and T. V. N. Persaud, *The Developing Human: Clinically Oriented Embryology, Eighth Edition*, page 272, Figure 12.37. Copyright © 2008 by Saunders, an imprint of Elsevier, Inc. Reprinted with the permission of Elsevier Science Limited.

Figure 4.1 From N. Wade, "Tug of War Pits Genes of Parents in the Fetus" from *The New York Times* (September 13, 2010): Section D, p. 5. Copyright © 2010 by The New York Times Company. All rights reserved. Used by permission. The printing, copying, redistribution, or retransmission of the Material without express written permission is prohibited.

Figure 4.2 From M. M. McCarthy and A. T. Konkle, "When is a sex difference not a sex difference?" from *Frontiers in Neuroendocrinology*, 26(2): 87, Figure 1. Copyright © 2005 by Elsevier. Reprinted with permission.

Figure 4.4

(a) Neonate fusiform gyrus:

From J. LeRoy Conel, *The Postnatal Development of the Human Cerebral Cortex* (Harvard University Press, 1939). Figure 135.

(b) Three-month fusiform gyrus:

From J. LeRoy Conel, *The Postnatal Development of the Human Cerebral Cortex* (Harvard University Press, 1947). Figure 147.

(c) Six-month fusiform gyrus:

From J. LeRoy Conel, *The Postnatal Development of the Human Cerebral Cortex* (Harvard University Press, 1951). Figure 147.

(d) Fifteen-month fusiform gyrus:

From J. LeRoy Conel, *The Postnatal Development of the Human Cerebral Cortex* (Harvard University Press, 1955). Figure 147.

Table 5.2 From M. Hines, S. F. Ahmed, and I. A. Hughes, "Psychological Outcomes and Gender-Related Development in Complete Androgen Insensitivity Syndrome" from *Archives of Sexual Behavior*, 32(2): 99–100, Appendix A. Copyright © 2003 by Springer Netherlands. Reprinted with the permission of Springer.

Table 5.3 After Rust, J., Golombok, S., Hines, M., Johnston, K., & Golding, J. (2000). The role of brothers and sisters in the gender development of preschool children. *Journal of Experimental Child Psychology*, 77(4), 292–303.

Figure 6.3 Geoffrey Warren, excerpt from *Fashion Accessories since 1500*. Copyright © 1987 by Geoffrey Warren. Reprinted with the permission of HarperCollins Publishers, Ltd.

Figures 6.4, 6.5, 6.7 Reprinted by permission of the publisher from *Brain Storm: The Flaws in the Science of Sex Differences* by Rebecca M. Jordan-Young, pp. 130, 141, 168, Cambridge, MA: Harvard University Press. Copyright © 2010 by the President and Fellows of Harvard College.

Figure 6.6 From E. O. Laumann, J. H. Gagnon, R. T. Michael and S. Michaels, *The Social Organization of Sexuality: Sexual Practices in the United States*. Copyright © 1994 by Edward O. Laumann, Robert T. Michael, CSG Enterprises, Inc., and Stuart Michaels. Reprinted with the permission of The University of Chicago Press.

Figure 7.1 Anne Fausto-Sterling with the aid of http://www.bolderstats.com/jmsl/doc/CohenD.htm

Table 7.2 From J. S. Hyde, "New Directions in the Study of Gender Similarities and Differences" from *Current Directions in Psychological Science*, 16 (2007): 260, Table 1. Copyright © 2007 by the Association for Psychological Science. Reprinted with the permission of Sage Publications, Inc.

Figure 7.2a From R. Lewontin, *Human Diversity*, p. 21. Copyright © 1982. Reprinted with the permission of W. H. Freeman and Company.

Figure 7.2b From C. D. Schlichting and M. Pigliucci, *Phenotypic Evolution: A Reaction Norm Perspective*, p. 56, Figure 3–5. Copyright © 1998. Reprinted with the permission of Sinauer Associates, Inc., Publishers.

INDEX

Note: Page numbers in **bold** are for figures, those in *italics* are for tables.